Global English for Global Business

Rachel McAlpine

LONGMAN

Addison Wesley Longman New Zealand Limited
46 Hillside Road, Auckland 10,
New Zealand

Associated companies throughout the world

First published 1997

ISBN 0 582 73998 5

Produced by Addison Wesley Longman New Zealand Limited
Printed in Malaysia through Longman Malaysia, TCP
Typeset in Palatino 10.5/12pt

We use **paper from sustainable forestry**

Contents

1

Global English: a secret code

We in the English-speaking world have often been highly complacent in expecting others to learn English without our making anything like the same effort in return.

Bill Bryson, *Mother Tongue*

This book will help you to write and speak English that your international clients can understand easily. *Global English for Global Business* explains how to adapt English to communicate with people who have a different mother tongue.

Using Global English is just as easy as using normal business English. And it is much easier than using complicated, ungrammatical English that nobody can understand. Global English consists of a few basic principles that can be adapted according to the situation. With practice, the Global English approach will become second nature.

Your company may be sending out letters and reports that are virtually incomprehensible to the receiver.

If you trade with non-English-speaking countries, your company needs a systematic Global English training and editing programme. Until that's in place, the success of your international communications will be random. Some staff members may certainly gain Global English skills on the job – either by happy accident or through cruel experience. Others are sublimely unconscious that their letters are contributing to your international communication problems. Under this regime, your company is pouring clients, time and money down the drain.

That international voice

Certain experienced diplomats, businesspeople and teachers of EFL (English as a foreign language) have cracked the secret code of international communication in English. When writing or speaking in an international environment, they automatically use short sentences, ask only one question at a time, and avoid idioms and negative expressions. They have learned the necessary tricks intuitively or by trial and error. I decided to systematise this secret code and train other people to use it. I have named the code Global English.

The seed for *Global English for Global Business* was sown shortly after I returned from two years in Japan as a visiting professor. A friend looked at me speculatively and observed, 'Your voice has changed. You've got that international voice.'

I knew exactly what he meant, though I'd never heard anyone else mention such a thing. In Japan I had often noticed people using a rather slow, precise and careful voice to speak English. Sometimes I couldn't tell whether they were American, British or Australian. You hear the same voice on radio and TV when certain people are interviewed after years abroad. They articulate clearly. They sound their final consonants: instead of running words together, they finish one word before they speak the next. They use short simple sentences. They've lost their local accents.

'That international voice' is a style of English that everyone can understand.

Strangely, two people from non-English-speaking countries may understand each other's English just fine – better than they understand an American or British person's speech. There are many reasons why this can happen. Probably both speakers learned English formally from similar books. They share the same vocabulary pool, and have been shielded from phrasal verbs, idiomatic English and complex sentence constructions. They are speaking Global English.

By contrast, many speeches to international audiences might as well be in Klingon language, for all the communication they achieve. Even world-famous academics often haul out the identical lecture they gave at Harvard or Cambridge, and repeat it without changing a word – regardless of what continent they're on. They make no effort to speak clearly or slowly. They make no allowance whatsoever for the fact that their audience is not fluent in English. Unfortunately, their audiences are usually too polite to show that they understand only a fraction of the English lecture or presentation.

Let us assume that these travelling English speakers are merely thoughtless, not arrogant. Certainly they are untrained in Global English. But I have a horrible suspicion their behaviour may be the norm.

There is an exact equivalent in written English. We run the risk of misjudging the reader's ability every time we write to someone whose mother tongue is not English. Good intentions are not enough. We need specific language skills before we can be confident that international clients will understand our English. *Global English for Global Business* provides the essential know-how.

TRY THIS

Why might international clients have trouble understanding the following sentence?

An apparent bungle by Obludu District Council planners has been identified as one of the key reasons why the Dianeville City Centre project could not kick off in time to take advantage of positive market forces, resulting in the Obludu New Enterprise Trust eventually finding itself in financial difficulties.

English is the conqueror

At the present time English... is the language in which the fate of most of the world's millions is decided.

Robert Phillipson

In the past, serious attempts have been made to create a language of international communication. First Latin and then French was regarded as a lingua franca. Then there was Esperanto, and then there was Basic English – another idealistic plan that never got off the ground.

Now the contest is over, and English has won. The English language dominates international communications in business, science and diplomacy. For largely historical reasons, English rules worldwide in print, on radio and TV, at conferences, and on the Internet.

There is concern about the way that English is conquering, colonising and corrupting other languages. Some non-English speakers resent the pressure to learn English. Users of most non-European languages are doubly disadvantaged, because they use a different script.

Commonly, native English speakers take the coloniser's attitude. 'If the non-English speakers of the world have trouble understanding us – they must raise the standard of their English. It's their problem, not ours.'

There's another way of looking at this. People born and bred into an English-speaking environment are hugely privileged. The rest of the world is making an immense effort to learn our language, and we can do our part by tailoring our international communications into Global English. That's a small gesture with a big impact.

But no ethical issues need enter the equation. We English speakers are literally losers if we write carelessly to international clients.

The high cost of not communicating clearly

One of the serious afflictions of International Communication Disorder is loss of business.

David L. James

Whenever a legitimate effort is made to count the cost of faulty communication, the statistics are positively frightening. English-speaking countries have communication problems on a grand scale.

- Australia: US $2.03 billion per year, plus US $10.29 million for industrial accidents
- Canada: US $2.38 billion per year
- Britain: US $13.65 billion per year.

When companies are dealing with international clients, the costs of poor communication escalate mightily. In 1987 the European Community found that translating its documents cost US $500 per page. A third of the EC's administration costs was spent on translators and interpreters, and in 1987 that meant US $700 million.

At the simplest level, wasting time is wasting money. If we have to write three letters instead of one, that is certainly wasting money. And we will often lose business in the process.

Get it right the first time

Every international document or speech must be written correctly the first time. When misunderstandings occur, untangling them can become a never-ending process.

Picture this common scenario. You send a letter to a client abroad.

The reply shows that the letter was misunderstood. So you write another letter to clarify the first one – thus doubling the amount of English material that your client must read. The international client deduces that you have changed the message, begins to distrust you, and breaks off negotiations.

International toll calls add to the cost of miscommunication – in more ways than one. In our own country, we'd pick up the phone to sort out most communication problems. Not so if your client is in a non-English-speaking country. Then the telephone can become an object of terror for both parties.

Often only a damage-control business trip to the country concerned can solve an international miscommunication problem.

We may have no idea that our efforts to communicate have failed. Why? Because the only sign is no sign. We receive no answer. Our letter is sitting in China or Russia in the file labelled 'Baffling Documents in the English Language'. We've lost that business forever, because our letter was not written in Global English.

Much worse are the occasions when a reader misinterprets a document and initiates legal proceedings. Need I say it? This can be costly.

Questions about Global English

England and America are two countries divided by a common language.

George Bernard Shaw

What is Global English?

Global English is a form of English that is customised and simplified for an international audience. In Global English you select words with care, structure your writing a particular way, and avoid other specific linguistic traps. Any document written in Global English will be grammatically correct and relatively easy for your international readers to understand.

Who should use Global English?

You should, if you need to communicate with people whose mother tongue is not English, or who don't hear English around them every day.

Your organisation should be using Global English if it is involved in any of the following:

- exporting of goods and services
- international consultancy
- travel and tourism
- study trips, student exchanges
- sister city arrangements
- immigration
- refugee management
- international conferences
- international aid.

I use normal English. Is that the same as Global English?

No. English is a rich, complex language full of subtleties and oddities and difficulties. Global English simplifies the particular elements that are hard for international readers to understand.

No matter where you live, your English is a local form of English. There is no such thing as standard English. You use many expressions and sentence constructions that are specific to your own area. Every location has its own local form of English – including Los Angeles, New York, Toronto, London, Glasgow, Brisbane, Auckland, Singapore, Johannesburg, Delhi and your own city.

I'm a really good writer. Why should I learn Global English?

I believe you! You may be a verbal, intelligent, informed and confident writer. For that very reason, it's very likely that some international readers can't understand your writing easily. You probably have a large vocabulary and are comfortable writing long sentences and expressing complex thoughts. The odds are that your natural writing is too academic or too unpredictable for easy comprehension.

I'm a reluctant writer. Why should I learn Global English?

Global English gives simple guidelines that will help you to write error-free English. Global English emphasises simplicity and consistency, and this is easy to achieve.

Isn't Global English an insult to the reader's intelligence?

Quite the reverse. Using Global English is a courteous gesture. Our normal business English may muddle, mislead and mystify international readers. Worse, it may irritate, alienate and humiliate them. These effects contribute to the hidden costs of international communication failure.

Is Global English necessary for all international communication in English?

Yes. If in any doubt about whether a client will comprehend your kind of English, follow the principles of Global English. And use Global English whenever you communicate with anyone who uses English in a different way from you.

How many people are we talking about?

Probably about one billion people use English as their second (or third or fourth...) language. That's about one quarter of the world's population. The numbers are growing rapidly: the British Council estimates that by the year 2000, one billion people will be learning English as a foreign language. In 1996 three million Chinese children began participating in an elementary school English programme – and that was just the pilot programme!

Why should I use Global English when I write to a bilingual person?

Assume that every document you send abroad will be copied and discussed at a meeting. Decisions are made communally in many foreign companies, especially in Asia. Thus it is likely that your documents will be read by a number of people, some of whom have minimal English.

And use Global English if your documents will be translated: Global English eliminates all the English usages that are difficult (or impossible) to translate.

Plain English seems fancy to some

If it can be misinterpreted, it will be misinterpreted.

Turner's law

The modern trend is to write business and legal documents in Plain English. That is a great blessing – within an English-speaking country. Unfortunately, Plain English has certain hazards for your international clients.

Some crucial differences exist between Plain English and Global English. The following sample sentence illustrates some of those differences.

Sample Plain English sentence

✖ I should very much like to get out to your head office soon, if that is not a problem for you.

The meaning of the sample sentence is pretty obvious to a person born in the USA, Britain, Australia or New Zealand. But here are 12 reasons why non-English speakers may find the sample sentence hard to understand.

The sample sentence is not Global English because it has:

1. 21 words: too many for Global English
2. 11 miniwords in a 21-word sentence: too high a proportion for Global English
3. a complex four-word verb form (should like to make)
4. a modal auxiliary verb with several possible meanings (should)
5. an adverbial phrase interrupting the main verb (very much)
6. a phrasal verb with several possible meanings (get out to)
7. a vague word (soon)
8. a colloquial expression (if that is not a problem for you)
9. a complex structure (main clause plus a subordinate clause)
10. an important courtesy point buried at the end, almost as an aside
11. a confusing negative expression (if that is not a problem)
12. an ambiguous pronoun (that).

A clear, simple Global English version of the sentence follows. (There are several possible versions, depending on the writer's intention and the exact situation.)

✔ I plan to visit your head office between 21 January and 24 January. Will these dates suit you?

Can your foreign clients understand your English easily?

The whole point of using Global English is to help foreign readers understand what we mean. Can they understand our English quickly? easily? without losing face? without losing concentration?

Consider how much of our clients' energy goes into the act of reading. How much energy remains for thinking about what they read?

Energy needed for reading	Energy available for thinking
100%	zero
80%	20%
50%	50%
20%	80%

Empathise with your international readers

Try to read the following texts. Notice your own reactions as you try to decipher these foreign scripts.

Το ζεστό αεράκι παρέσυρε μια τούφα απ' τα μαλλιά της Άμπερ και την έριξε στο πρόσωπό της. Κάτω απ' το εκτυφλωτικό φως του καλοκαιριάτικου ήλιου της Νέας Ζηλανδίας, τα πλούσια σγουρά μαλλιά της έπαιρναν τις ανταύγειες του μελιού, που κυλούσε πάνω σε χρυσοκάστανο μετάξι, στο ηλιοκαμένο δέρμα της. Χρυσό κορίτσι

사나이의 훤칠한 키가 클래리의 주의를 끌었다. 황갈색 머리칼이 영국 북유의 차가운 햇살 속에서도 번쩍번쩍 빛나 보였다.

갑자기 박수소리가 일었다. 키 큰 사나이에게 정신이 팔려 있던 클래리는 재 정신으로 돌아왔다. 그리곤 승마장에

Camilla právě napouštěla vodu do vany v koupelně, když uslyšela telefon. Na okamžik zaváhala. Okres Bowden byl skoro poslední na Novém Zélandu, kde telefonní linky byly ještě společné a zvonění se podobalo jedno druhému. Dvojí dlouhé zvonění, které patřilo jí, se dalo lehce splést s jedním krátkým a dvěma

McAlpine 先生は，詩人，小説家，戯曲家であり，その他さまざまな分野において，執筆活動されている．既に出版されてた作品も多数ある．今年 4 月より，同志社女子大学で Creative Writing の指導をされている．

Naturally we can't understand these texts unless we are fluent in the particular languages. That's not surprising – yet our international clients often feel ashamed of their own inability to understand English well. With Global English we can help to ease that anxiety. The McAlpine EFLAW® Readability Index is the first step.

The McAlpine EFLAW® Readability Index

EFL = English as a Foreign Language

FLAW = imperfection, blemish; invalidating defect in documents, etc.

The McAlpine EFLAW® Readability Index measures how readable a document is to readers whose mother tongue is not English. Global English readability is based on two basic factors: the number of words and the number of miniwords per sentence. Miniwords are defined as words of one, two or three letters. (Chapters Two and Three explain why long sentences and miniwords in English documents create difficulties for international clients.)

Among the various problems that plague international communication, long sentences and miniwords loom very large. If we do just two things – use short sentences and a minimum of miniwords – many other flaws evaporate automatically.

Excessively long sentences and too many miniwords are signs that other flaws are present, such as difficult sentence constructions, negatives and phrasal verbs – all of which bring problems for people whose mother tongue is not English. This is why the McAlpine EFLAW® Readability Index concentrates exclusively on miniwords and sentence length.

With its focus on miniwords, the McAlpine EFLAW® Readability Index is fundamentally different from any other readability index you may be familiar with. (When writing for native English speakers, long words – not short words – are the problem.)

Note that the McAlpine EFLAW® Readability Index has not yet been scientifically tested. Please regard it as a quick, easy, approximate measure of international readability. After using the McAlpine EFLAW® Readability Index a few times, you'll be able to see at a glance whether a sentence needs changing. You'll learn, for example, that if a sentence runs over two lines, and has many little words, it's certain to have a high EFLAW® score.

How to use the McAlpine EFLAW® Readability Index

Remember, the fewer the flaws, the lower the EFLAW® score.

To establish the EFLAW® score of a document or paragraph

count the words	
count the miniwords	
add the two	(A)
count the sentences	(B)
divide (A) by (B)	(EFLAW® score)

A good EFLAW® score is under 25

EFLAW® score	EFL reader's response	
40	✖✖✖	This is too difficult. I won't read it.
35	✖✖	I'm struggling....
30	✖	I need a dictionary.
25	✔	This is OK.
20	✔✔	Fine! I can understand this.
15	✔✔✔	This is easy to read. I'll reply today.

TRY THIS

What is the EFLAW® score of the following passage?

Greatly attracted by the notion of having other people who pay themselves well to know what they are doing work for me (well, that's the theory), I have invested modestly in the sharemarket in recent times.

2

Choose the right words

What do you read, my Lord?
Words, words, words.
William Shakespeare

Words are the raw material of communication in Global English. As native English speakers we toss English words around without a second thought – often just for fun. We all have a different and very personal idea of what the word 'fun' means, and we don't have to consult a dictionary for the meaning.

This is not how it is for our international clients. When communicating with them in English, we have to think a bit harder before deciding which words to use. We have to visualise their environment. Sensitivity to their needs starts at the most fundamental level, with the very words we choose.

They'll probably rely on a bilingual dictionary. In a dictionary, longer words are easier to decipher than short, common words, and pronouns present a particular challenge. These points are specific to Global English.

This chapter also deals with the F-word problems. These are not unique to Global English, but they are particularly important for international communication.

Choose words with one clear meaning

Words strain,
Crack and sometimes break, under the burden...
T.S. Eliot

When we lucky native English speakers meet a word we don't understand, it's not a problem. We guess. We pick up clues from context. We can understand a phrase without fussing over the individual words. We are often satisfied with a vague idea of the meaning of a new phrase.

That's not how our international clients function. They usually consult a bilingual dictionary. They get stumped if the word isn't in the dictionary, or if the word has too many alternative meanings in the dictionary.

Therefore it's best to choose words that are likely to be in a bilingual dictionary, and that have a limited number of dictionary meanings.

Choosing words with one clear meaning is not a matter of choosing easy words. Native English speakers use easy words like 'get' with confidence, and may hesitate before using a difficult word like 'microcosmic'. For our international clients, 'microcosmic' is simple: a bilingual dictionary quickly reveals the meaning. But consulting a dictionary for the meaning of 'get' can add to the confusion, because 'get' has at least 100 common meanings.

What do we mean by 'words with one clear meaning'? First, to state the obvious, they have only one meaning – not two or more meanings. Take the word 'fair', for instance, in this sentence: 'Mrs Jackson is a fair woman.' We can guess from the context that 'fair' means 'unbiased'. But the sentence has the potential to confuse, because 'fair' can also mean 'beautiful', 'blonde', 'considerable', 'satisfactory' or 'of moderate quality'.

In Global English the words 'as', 'while' and 'since' all have at least two meanings. One meaning is related to time, and one is related to contrast or cause and effect. Would your international clients understand the difference between the next two sentences? In the first sentence, 'since' means 'after' and in the second, 'since' means 'because'.

✖ Since the government promised increased spending, building industry shares have soared.

✖ Since the government has promised increased spending, building industry shares have soared.

To avoid possible confusion it is often simplest to rewrite sentences, getting rid of 'as', 'while' and 'since'.

✖ As Cyclone Drena's track will cross Northland, campers are being evacuated.

✔ Because Cyclone Drena's track will travel across Northland, campers are being evacuated.

✖ While sales of perfume in France rose by 2-3% last year, exports have risen by up to 10%.

✔ Sales of perfume in France rose by 2-3% last year. By contrast, exports of perfume rose by up to 10%.

The ideal words for Global English have meanings that are specific and definite. Many words we use in everyday life have a rather vague meaning. How about 'community'? In an international context this may be too vague to grasp. If you mean 'clubs and schools', say that. If you mean 'the ratepayers of Toowoomba', say that.

The best words for Global English make sense alone, out of context. 'Voters' always means 'voters', so that's a good Global English word. But 'grassroots' can mean either 'voters' or 'fundamental level or source' or, presumably, the roots of a grass plant. Also, 'voters' is more likely to be in a bilingual dictionary than 'grassroots'.

Check that the words you choose are in a standard dictionary, or even better, in a bilingual dictionary.

TRY THIS

Change one word to make the meaning of this sentence clearer.

The conference facilities are free on 23–24 July.

Miniwords confuse international readers

Examples of English miniwords

to, of, in, out, at, for, up, by, on, off, yet, or, but, for, and, nor, not, if, as, not, how, so, the, a, I, you, we, he, she, it, who, get, put, go, do, put, sit, was, is, may, can, will

Why should miniwords be such a bother for people from a non-English-speaking background? (By miniwords I mean words of three letters or fewer.)

A miniword is likely to be one (or more) of the following:

- very common – so common that the dictionary has many, many meanings for that word
- a pronoun – and pronouns are potentially confusing
- a virtually meaningless structural word like 'a' or 'of'.

Almost every language has its equivalent of thorny little miniwords. No matter what language we are learning, it's the little things that trip us up, and the miniwords are deadly.

Learning French, we have no trouble with *plume* and *livre* – it's *le* and *la* that bamboozle us. (Why should a pen be feminine and a book be masculine?) These French miniwords have no equivalent in English.

In Japanese, English speakers wrestle with *ga* and *wa*. *Wa* means 'as for' or 'talking about' – or does it? *Wa* often signals the subject of the sentence – but not always. *Ga* emphasises the subject – or does it? The wrong use of the miniwords is a dead giveaway: native speakers don't make these mistakes.

The same is true of English. When people are learning English, the miniwords can seem very weird, and cause a disproportionate amount of trouble.

Your international clients may read English slowly, word by word. But English is a language of phrases, and many miniwords make no sense at all except within a phrase. Your aim therefore in Global English is to select words that make sense alone, and to keep the proportion of miniwords low.

About structural words and meaningful words

English words can be divided roughly into two types: meaningful words and structural words.

Meaningful words are words with a self-contained meaning, like 'pen' and 'book'. They are comparatively easy to grasp. The majority of meaningful words have at least four letters.

Structural words connect the meaningful words together to form phrases and sentences. (Many structural words are miniwords.)

Window cleaning **is a** mysterious science.

I learnt **the** wily ways **of** window cleaning **in** Sydney.

Meaningful words should predominate in Global English. Meaningful words alone can often carry the essential meaning. This sometimes happens in headlines:

WOMAN BITES HORSE

WEARABLE ART STUNS AUDIENCE

At the beginning and end of life we manage just fine without structural words. Babies use only meaningful words at first. 'Milk!'

is a perfectly clear message, coming from a baby. By the same token, a person may lose the structural words after a stroke. One of the last things my mother said before she died was 'Lost prepositions. Most distressing!' Her meaning and her feelings were very clear, even though she had indeed lost her prepositions.

Why your clients may find structural words difficult

- Their own language may have no equivalent to the English structural words.
- Their own language may put structural words in different places.
- Structural words are hard to translate.

A high proportion of structural words is often a sign of woolly thinking. Structural words have little or no meaning, or else they have many meanings, or they subtly alter the tone of a sentence. So let's try and cut out the clutter.

Some examples follow. (See Fluffy Phrases later in this chapter for more examples.)

✖ Many structural words	✔ Fewer structural words
on the assumption that	we assume that
it would be appreciated if you would	please
in the event that	if
in respect of	about
by means of	by
for the purpose of	to
due to the fact that	because
is inclusive of	includes

TRY THIS

Rewrite the following sentence with fewer structural words.

It is a requirement that you should be certain to return this form.

Problems with pronouns

Question: What is your Name? Answer: N. or M.

The Catechism

Examples of pronouns

I, me, you, she, her, he, him, it, we, us, they, them, who, whom, what, this, that, these, those, my, mine, your, yours, his, hers, its, our, ours, their, theirs

Pronouns can be confusing, because readers must guess at identities. Some languages use very few pronouns. In other languages, pronouns refer not to a person's sex but to a person's status. So using English pronouns can be a waste of time.

The following sentence has four pronouns. 'I' and 'you' are clear enough. But who is 'him'? and what is 'it'? Non-English speakers need more help.

I'd like **you** to give **it** to **him**.

The following version is better for international readers.

Please give the folder to Mr Johnson.

Removing pronouns often means repeating nouns. That's OK. In fact, it's excellent, because repetition is a virtue in Global English. Key words are like signposts, providing context. (There's more about repeating key nouns in Chapter Eight.)

TRY THIS

christie has only one apple.

Change this sentence so that the meaning is clear.

This is the last one she has got.

This is the last apple christie has.

Avoid the F-words

Oh frabjous day! Calloo, callay!

Lewis Carroll

The following section is a reminder about the type of words we should avoid in all business English, whether for home or abroad. The only difference is that in Global English we have to be twice as careful to avoid them.

The F-words and phrases are fluffy ones, fuddy-duddy ones, fashionable ones and fancy ones.

Avoid fluffy phrases

Fluffy phrases are phrases overloaded with miniwords. They are hard to understand, hard to translate, and often a sign of illogical thought.

Example

In real terms this is not in fact a tax cut at all.

Rewritten in Global English without the fluffy phrases, this sentence becomes 'This is not a tax cut' or 'This is not a real tax cut'.

TRY THIS

Rewrite without the fluffy phrases.

There is a bit of a boredom factor creeping in.

Avoid fashionable words and phrases

English is changing all the time. Changes sneak up on us. It seems like only yesterday that we had never heard of 'outsourcing' or 'reengineering'.

Try to avoid using words and phrases that have recently become fashionable. They often have a new meaning, or a slightly strange meaning, or a vague meaning, or several different meanings. Indeed, fashionable phrases often mean all things to all people.

A person from a non-English-speaking background can only guess what these expressions mean. We can't assume that our international clients understand the new meaning of fashionable words. We can't even assume our clients use the latest dictionary – do you?

The words below have become fashionable comparatively recently. But what do they actually mean?

enhance

arguably

facilitate

clustering

debottlenecking

Words are forever escaping from the cage of the dictionary. For example, the correct meaning of 'adjacent' is 'next to'. Nowadays, a surprising number of people believe that it means 'opposite'. Check and double-check the meaning of words, even when you are sure you are right. Be certain that you are using words in their dictionary sense.

How about 'facilitate'? Its dictionary meaning is 'make easy, promote, help forward'. But when I ask English-speaking businesspeople what they think it means, I receive all manner of answers, including 'chair', 'teach', 'implement', 'fulfil', or 'communicate'.

Similarly, English-speaking people use 'parameter' to mean just about anything they like, including 'area', 'boundary', 'perimeter', 'value', 'condition', 'scope', 'rule', 'control' or 'volume'. I'm not criticising: it's interesting to observe the way that words are changing under our very noses. But you can see that for a person who is not exposed to English every day, fashionable words are a problem.

Slang is the ultimate in fashionable English, and it has no place in Global English. Global English requires a rather formal tone.

Slang changes from city to city, from social group to social group, and from month to month. Consider the phrase 'going off', for example. In 1995 it meant 'going rotten' in the North Island of New Zealand, whereas in the South Island it meant 'proceeding successfully'.

Slang deliberately excludes people who are not in our group. The following two sentences are incomprehensible to non-English speakers.

✖ Bay of Islands man on to it. Professional, 45 yrs old who loves the Lord seeks tall on to it feminine attractive lady.

✖ Nick has POGOed on to the gruesome Neo-Punk bandwagon, fronting the RAWK equivalent of an armpit fart.

Avoid fuddy-duddy words and phrases

At the other extreme, old-fashioned words and phrases are not suitable for Global English. Business writing throws up some peculiar phrases that have lingered on and refuse to die.

Examples

albeit (yes, I know Princess Diana uses this word, but it's still fuddy-duddy)

notwithstanding

we are in receipt of your letter of

as per your letter

we trust the foregoing is of assistance

should you have any queries please do not hesitate to contact the writer

Many people use these fussy, unnatural, old-fashioned clichés in business English – why? They do it because other people do it, which is not a good reason.

If you still use this sort of phrase, do stop and think about its effect on your international clients. It's very satisfying to find a new way of saying these things. Once you get used to it, writing naturally is easier than writing the fuddy-duddy way.

Think before using fancy words

Winnie-the-Pooh said, 'I am a Bear of Very Little Brain, and long words bother me.' Not so with your international clients! Long words won't necessarily bother them, provided they are in a bilingual dictionary. But rare or fancy words may certainly bother them.

How do we get it right? We are communicating with an intelligent person, perhaps with specialist knowledge, perhaps knowing several languages. Nevertheless that person's experience of the English language is different from ours.

Before using a difficult word, it's best to consult the dictionary. If the word's meaning isn't clear (or if it's not in the dictionary) – we can either explain the word's meaning, or use a simpler word.

Of course technical words have their place. For example, the following words are certainly too fancy for non-technical readers, yet for non-English speakers with the appropriate expertise, the meaning is obvious.

chimera, infrastructure, goniometer, nexus, flamefest, escrow, ergonomics, cline

TRY THIS

Rewrite the following sentence in Global English, making the meaning clear.

Out in the world we are so used to the council shouting down from the moral high-ground of environmental rectitude, we forget it might just be right.

3

Exploit the mighty verb

Verb the adjectival noun!

Profanity uttered by the Reverend D. M. Taylor

This chapter explains how verbs can make or break the comprehension of people from a non-English-speaking background.

In English, verbs are the go-go-go words, the wake-up words. In any sentence the verb is the turning point of meaning. There's no action until we hit that verb. So it's very important to make the most of verbs, to use their full potential for bringing clarity.

There are two major hazards with English verbs for people learning English. First, English phrasal verbs are a famous stumbling block. This chapter shows how to replace phrasal verbs with one-word verbs.

A second important problem for our international clients is the little helping verbs like 'must', 'should' or 'can'.

Another problem to avoid is separating the various parts of the verb.

Despite these problems, using a high proportion of verbs in Global English is highly recommended. Verbs (especially simple action verbs) help our international clients to get the message.

Use more verbs and fewer nouns

Just do it!

Nike slogan

Verbs bring action. Verbs make things happen. Nouns just add names of things.

When we use far more nouns than verbs, our writing has a heavy, dead feeling. Nothing is happening! People from a non-English-speaking background may feel as if they are stumbling around in a dictionary, crashing their shins on things, things, things.

In Global English, use verbs liberally. Not just any old verbs: use action verbs.

Use action verbs

Obviously the following verbs are action verbs, because we can 'see' some action happening when we read them:

to jump, run, collapse, explode, fry, fly, flee, flop, float, fling, parapent

But verbs don't have to be Outward Bounders to qualify as action verbs. The following are also action verbs:

to answer, inquire, investigate, cooperate, say, possess, confuse, rewrite, find, configure, spend, inaugurate, provide, reply

Action verbs convey the sense that somebody is doing something. Action verbs are easy to understand because they:

- can usually be visualised
- enforce clarity
- bring a sense of reality.

Other verbs, by contrast, merely suggest a state of existence, or a condition. When our language speeds up with action verbs, so does our international client's comprehension.

TRY THIS

Which two sentences contain action verbs.

1 The Council's stipulation was for industrial zoning.
2 The Council zoned the area industrial.
3 They are suffering from malnutrition.
4 Malnutrition is widespread.

Use verbs instead of abstract nouns

Abstract nouns refer to things we cannot clearly visualise, like 'peace', 'corruption', 'enforcement' or 'philosophy'. Understanding abstract nouns is a triumph of the human brain. Grappling with more than one abstract noun in a sentence is a challenge, even in our own language – and for people working in a different language, it is asking too much.

Non-English speakers are already performing mental gymnastics when they read or listen to English. We can help them by using words they can visualise. The more clearly our international clients can visualise what we say, the more easily they'll understand. So wherever possible, use a verb instead of an abstract noun.

✔ **Verbs**: consider, sense, construct, adjust

✖ **Abstract nouns**: consideration, sensitivity, construction, adjustment

Words with the following endings are usually abstract nouns:

-ment, -ion, -tion, -ance, -ment, -ence, -ance, -ancy, -ency, -ity, -ism

Example

The following sentence is full of abstract nouns:

✖ In conjunction with the alleviation of pain there is an expectation of a diminution of body temperature.

Here's the same sentence in Global English, with the nouns turned into verbs:

✔ We expect that body temperature will fall and pain will diminish.

TRY THIS

Rewrite this sentence in Global English, replacing one or two of the abstract nouns with verbs.

There has been a significant reduction in reported crime in Crumpville which is in direct opposition to the national trend.

Phrasal verbs are a nightmare for non-English speakers

This is the type of arrant pedantry up with which I will not put.
Winston Churchill

Phrasal verbs are two- or three-word verbs. They consist of an ordinary verb combined with one or two structural words like 'in' or 'out' or 'off'. Phrasal verbs are notoriously difficult for people learning English – so difficult that special dictionaries of phrasal verbs are necessary. Over 3000 phrasal verbs are in common use in everyday modern English.

Examples of phrasal verbs

break into, break out, break up, break away, break down, break off

put in, put off, put away, put about, put on, put up, put over, put out

run in, run into, run up, run off, run out of, run over, run by

blow out, blow up, blow away, blow over, blow back

TRY THIS

Replace each of the following phrasal verbs with one word.

1 let out
2 give up surrender
3 come along with accompany
4 give away give

It's hard to find the meanings of phrasal verbs in a dictionary

Have mercy on your international clients. They may have very few phrasal verbs in their vocabulary pool. When they read a phrasal verb, they must consult a dictionary. And in the dictionary they find very long entries with multiple meanings for the phrasal verb. Seeking the meaning of phrasal verbs wastes a lot of time.

The verb 'to get' is typical of the commonest English verbs. Imagine consulting a dictionary looking for the meaning of 'get'. The avalanche of phrasal verbs in a dictionary could overwhelm someone whose mother tongue is not English.

get about	get above
get across	get after
get ahead	get along
get around	get around to
get at	get away
get away from	get away with
get back	get back at
get back into	get back to
get behind	get beyond
get by	get down

continued...

get down to	get in
get in on	get into
get in with	get off
get off on	get off with
get on	get on at
get on for	get on to
get out	get out of
get over	get over with
get round	get round to
get through	get to
get together	get up
get up to	get with
get it into one's head	get his, theirs
get it	have got to
get with child	get well, get better
get-rich-quick	get outside of

Just finding a particular phrasal verb in the dictionary is only the start of your client's woes. Any one of those phrasal verbs has numerous meanings. For example, *The Concise Oxford Dictionary* has 16 different usages for the phrasal verb 'to put up'.

22. ~up, construct, build; raise (price, etc.); offer (prayer), present (petition, proposal), provide (money as backer, etc.); propose, be candidate, for election; cause (game) to rise from cover; publish (banns); offer for sale or competition; pack up in a parcel or receptacle; sheathe (sword); lodge (guest), be or become lodger at; concoct (~-up a., fraudulently concocted); put person's BACK up; put up a FIGHT; put one's HAIR up; ~up to, inform (person) of, instruct (person) in, instigate (person) in (doing, etc.); ~ up with, submit to, tolerate, (annoyance, insult, etc.).

Many of the definitions of the phrasal verb 'to put' are one-word verbs with one clear meaning. Notice that most of the one-word verbs are longer words, slightly more formal than 'put up'.

construct – build – raise – offer – sheathe – present – provide –propose – cause – publish – concoct – inform – instruct – instigate – tolerate

Use one-word verbs in Global English

Japan has a god called Hitokotonushi-no-kami – the God of One Word.

A sensible rule is to replace all phrasal verbs with one-word verbs when you write Global English. (The dictionary often provides a good alternative.)

For your international clients, the meaning of a one-word verb (like 'construct') is easy to find in a dictionary.

Dictionary entry for one-word verb 'construct'	5 lines
Dictionary entry for phrasal verb 'put up'	14 lines
Dictionary entry for 'put'	135 lines

TRY THIS

Rewrite, using one-word verbs instead of phrasal verbs.

I will check up on the programme, look over the timetable and get on with the reservations.

Beware of moody little helping verbs

I would if I could but I can't.

All the moody little helping verbs (modal auxiliary verbs) are difficult for our international clients to interpret correctly. We should eliminate them whenever possible in Global English.

Modal auxiliary verbs are words like:

am	could
do	may
will	might
would	shall
can	should

These little helpers hint at the mood of the writer: is this something that may happen, might happen, should happen, can happen, could happen, must happen or will happen? The moody little helpers give us a clue.

Native English speakers create complicated verbs using a basic verb plus a few helpers. Some of these helpers are fairly straightforward – for example 'do', 'does', 'am', 'is', 'are', 'was' and 'were'. But even these can confuse an international client.

Moody helping verbs can change the mood of an English sentence in ways that are arbitrary, illogical or excruciatingly subtle. Native English speakers use these words almost interchangeably, relying on context to convey their meaning. But context hints are far too subtle for many people who did not grow up in an English-speaking environment.

Were you taught how to differentiate between 'shall' and 'will', 'should' and 'would'? Bad luck – knowing the rules is no use today. The modal auxiliaries have developed into a grammatical brat pack, meaning whatever they will (or would or want or must).

Don't trust the moody little helper verbs. Instead, think seriously about what you mean. Then, provide specific words that convey the mood or tense of your verb, such as 'we recommend', 'possibly', 'you must', 'in the future', or 'please'. These help to show what mood you are in.

Rephrasing a sentence can make our intention absolutely clear. Reading English is quite hard enough for your international clients: don't expect them to read your mood as well.

Below are some examples of how to clarify the mood of a verb.

✖ Ambiguous	✔ Clear
I am going to Seoul.	I have decided to travel to Seoul.
I will be coming next week.	I intend to come on Tuesday.
I won't leave San Francisco.	I refuse to leave San Francisco. I intend to remain in San Francisco.
The CEO does agree with you.	The CEO definitely agrees with you.
Mr West is to sign the treaty soon.	Mr West will sign the treaty on 23 May 1998.
You can do this.	You are capable of doing this. It is possible for you to do this. You are entitled to do this.
Can you open a window please?	Please open a window.
Could you open a window?	Please open a window.
They could do this.	They are capable of doing this. Possibly they will do this. We believe they will do this. They have several options. One option is to do this.
You may do this.	You are permitted to do this. You are entitled to do this. Perhaps you will do this.
He might visit Asia.	Maybe he will visit Asia.

continued...

✖ Ambiguous	✔ Clear
If I might have a copy...	Please send me a copy.
Should you do this....	If you do this....
If you should do this....	If you do this...
You should do this.	Please do this.
	This is preferable.
	We advise you to do this.
	You must do this.
	This is mandatory.
I shall do this.	I intend to do this.
	I am determined to do this.
They shall do this.	They must do this.
	They are legally required to do this.

TRY THIS

Write the following sentences so that your mood is absolutely clear to a non-English speaker. (There are several possible answers.)

1 We will do this.

2 I would if I could but I can't.

Keep all the bits of a verb together

Another hazard is splitting up the bits and pieces of a verb. This is tough on people who are not accustomed to using English. Short simple verbs are best, but sometimes we have to write a verb consisting of several words. In these cases, keep the main elements of every verb together.

✖ Examples of interrupted verbs

is quietly weeping

was, while climbing, injured

will shortly be sued

should according to the schedule have departed

✔ The same verbs with their bits united

is weeping quietly

was injured while climbing

will be sued shortly

should have departed, according to the schedule

TRY THIS

Rewrite this sentence as two shorter sentences. Keep the bits of each verb together.

Albatross Aviation has been continuously operating for over 20 years, and is, according to CEO Susan Dufresne, about to acquire three more twin-engined planes.

4

Remove mysterious metaphors

Metaphor... is not just a device for adding colour: it is a process by which language is constantly refreshed.
Nicholas Hudson

For people with a different mother tongue, the idioms of English are confusing in the extreme. We just use certain expressions because we have always heard them said that way. No logical rules apply. We can't explain them.

Our language is saturated with metaphors, where one thing is compared with another. 'Shall I compare thee to a summer's day?' mused Shakespeare. An original metaphor is fresh and new. If people start using it often, the metaphor becomes an idiom, and eventually a stale old cliché. Then we don't even notice we are using language metaphorically. For our international clients, this can be highly disconcerting. They need to 'translate' a metaphor twice: once into the literal meaning, and once into their own language.

'I heard it on the grapevine' is a metaphor meaning 'Somebody told me'. 'We've got our ear to the ground' means 'We're alert to news and rumours'. But how is somebody learning English supposed to guess that?

There is little logic to English idiom. Why 'the tip of the iceberg'? Why 'hard business networks'? Why the 'trickle down' effect? And how are English learners expected to decipher mixed metaphors, like the following examples?

✖ Things are starting to jell, and maybe we're going to peak at the right time.

✖ The bottom line is, we are pinning our hopes on adding value downstream.

In Global English, try very, very hard to avoid idioms and other hidden metaphors. And then double-check and try even harder. If we use idiomatic language unfamiliar to our clients, they will take the meaning literally.

A certain businessman had just completed negotiations with a Chinese exporting company. With satisfaction he closed the meeting with the words, 'So it will all be plain sailing from now on!' This flustered his Chinese colleagues: they thought he meant all the goods would be sent by sea.

How to detect a hidden metaphor

> **metaphor:** *calling one thing by the name of another, explicitly or implicitly, for purposes of comparison, e.g. using 'to fly' to mean to hurry away; calling a treacherous person a 'snake'.*
>
> Derek Wallace and Janet Hughes

Visualise the scene conveyed by the phrases below. What do these phrases mean literally? Do you 'see' a picture of something irrelevant or crazy?

- a steep learning curve (a student going up a steep hill to university?)
- a step in the right direction (someone stepping to the right?)
- at the end of the day (sunset?)
- pave the way for (someone laying paving stones?)

TRY THIS

What might an international client think the following metaphors mean?

1. just around the corner
2. on the horizon
3. before the tax cut kicks in
4. right across the spectrum
5. gearing up.

The scale of the problem is massive

> *...repetition in itself increases the probability of repetition. In other words, the more times a 'mental event' happens, the more likely it is to happen again.*
>
> Tony Buzan

Hidden metaphors are not just an occasional or rare problem for clients trying to understand English. Metaphors are a fundamental characteristic of English, and probably of all human thinking. All learning depends on association. We learn by hooking a new concept or experience to our memory of something we know already. (Indeed, Marcel Proust claimed that we cannot actually experience a sensation until we have linked it to another sensation with a metaphor.) We can look upon metaphor as a linguistic manifestation of a neuronal embrace.

There is no way we could eliminate metaphor from the English language, because metaphor exists for a neurophysiological reason. Moreover, metaphor epitomises the colour and glamour and energy and poetry of our language. Language is metaphor!

So it is hardly surprising that we use metaphor and idiom almost every time we open our mouths or hit the keyboard.

Obviously, therefore, we cannot regard hidden metaphors and idiom as a trivial problem of international communication. This is a colossal problem that can overwhelm people as they struggle to understand English.

To discover just how commonly hidden metaphors occur in our language, I listened to a single hour of radio on 1 October 1996. The programme was Morning Report on New Zealand's National Radio, an essentially conservative, mainstream news programme. Speakers were hosts Geoff Robinson and Mike Smith, plus various reporters and interviewees including two Ministers of the Crown. I wrote down all the hidden metaphors I heard in that hour. They poured out – I could hardly write fast enough to catch them all.

1 southwesterlies dying out
2 on the smell of an oily rag
3 in the end they took what they could get
4 the march is part of a bid to get
5 the lakes generate $42 million annually
6 the Minister is singing the praises of Maori health workers
7 they were going over how to recognise symptoms

8 they were keen to get on with something
9 it wasn't going to turn around many years of disadvantage in a year
10 the debts run up by patients
11 the government was toppled last night
12 a sitting of Parliament
13 to lodge a protest
14 kept up blockades
15 a round-up of opposition protesters
16 to launch a major crackdown
17 the LDC takes a hard line on the northern islands
18 at the centre of protests
19 Mr Toma has been tracked down
20 there's been a call for him to step down
21 investors were heartened
22 the bond market dipped
23 the DOW has been strong
24 the robust report
25 in line with economists' forecast
26 a firmness in the US economy
27 may lend weight to a call to cut interest rates
28 it's not a done deal yet
29 Prime Minister Jim Bolger is shrugging off criticism
30 he is a bad loser
31 he is trying to take the economy down on his way out
32 the latest poll points to a continued rise in the fortunes of Labour
33 with Labour cementing itself into second place
34 still trails the Prime Minister in popularity
35 why did the market fall so steeply?
36 the market is driven by the flow of orders
37 hot money
38 lighten up their exposure
39 they're down to the bone now
40 cash continues to build up
41 a left-wing coalition government

42 be mindful of
43 gold is well back
44 life on the beat
45 Bill Clinton's big gamble on the Middle East
46 police continue to scour the Horowhenua district
47 the hospital was out of pocket
48 Samoan patients topped the list
49 they are up for a third of the debt
50 officials are working on the problem
51 there are mixed feelings
52 positive spin-off for the whole community
53 a settlement will go ahead
54 take some of the diplomatic pressure off
55 without addressing the underlying problems
56 if the government won't move on the issue
57 students have been absorbing the additional cost
58 students are taking up the slack
59 police are defending their handling of the Bain homicide case
60 is still on the run
61 the 1300-strong workforce
62 management turning a blind eye
63 they were all within the fiscal envelope
64 the cash and land package
65 Whaka Tohia lost their land
66 we had 100 people killed by the Crown
67 fulfil their place in society
68 no longer be marginalised
69 in good faith
70 this isn't binding
71 take up the cudgels
72 seek the passage through Parliament
73 for five years on and off, mostly on
74 no use getting downcast
75 we have to grin and bear it

76 it's probably 50-50
77 made up the bulk of a multimillion dollar debt
78 ripping off the system
79 that sounds like fraud
80 we should get these people
81 are you standing for Parliament?
82 questions about the Bain trial just will not go away
83 to back up Coghill's claim
84 at the end of the day
85 he deserves a fair go
86 the tip of the iceberg
87 it's not for me to say.

Use language literally, not metaphorically

> *Inherently promiscuous, language is divided by a fragile barrier separating carefully contained expression from the perverse screams of a madman.*
>
> Clark Lunberry

Every one of the expressions in the list above is capable of causing a misunderstanding with an international client. At best the client may have to consult a dictionary. At worst he or she may infer an entirely false meaning. Yet these are all everyday expressions – things we might say or write without a second thought.

Relentless vigilance is necessary to avoid using such phrases. We can sensitise ourselves so that we always notice when we use an idiomatic or metaphoric phrase in our international communications. Then we can eliminate or explain them.

If the following Web page was intended for a worldwide readership, it should have been heavily edited. Count the hidden metaphors: there are at least nine. Even the mysterious metaphorical title would slow down the reading speed of many people from a non-English-speaking background.

'Feeding Our Community the Dream of a Future'

| Home | Sponsors | Recipes | Chefs | non-Profits | Donate |

Want to help build the future of society?

If you...

Care about kids

Think computers are important to the future of the world

Like food

...then you are in the right place. Kids are the building blocks of the future, and Cookin' aims to feed knowledge to those who often can't afford the meal ticket. Cookin' On The Net is an Internet-based charity effort designed to raise funds for non-profits who are helping to connect disadvantaged kids with computer resources and technology.

You can make a difference right now!! For an electronic donation of just $12, you can help get computer technology into the hands of kids from five U.S. cities... and enjoy five recipes from some of America's leading chefs.

As an added bonus, we also have some CDs from Windham Hill and cookbooks from Warner Books that you can register to win. So don't just sit there, jump in...

TRY THIS

Rewrite these sentences to eliminate the hidden metaphors and make their meaning absolutely clear.

1 Our client has been done justice to by the book.
2 It is our policy to assist fledgling languages to find their feet and gain momentum.
3 You can't flog product on the first visit.
4 They're crying out for finished leather.
5 Without great creative hooks, commented an experienced ad man, what have you got to hang your hat on?

5

Use short sentences

I told them once, I told them twice:
They would not listen to advice.
Lewis Carroll

Short sentences are a supreme advantage when communicating with people from a non-English-speaking background. If you want your English to be understood worldwide – write short sentences. If you want to avoid embarrassing grammar mistakes and excruciating international misunderstandings – use short sentences. If you want your international clients to read your documents easily, confidently and accurately – use short sentences. Short sentences are the bottom line of Global English.

I'm going to say that one more time. 'Write short sentences.' Did everybody hear?

By 'short' sentences, I mean a maximum of 20 words. And whenever possible, write sentences of 16 words or fewer.

The benefits mount up as we follow this rule. In fact, if we systematically write short sentences, then many international communication problems automatically vanish.

You can tell at a glance if a written sentence is too long. Note how many words per line appear on your computer screen or on the printed page. Does the 20-word quota occupy two lines? one-and-a-half lines? Keep tuned to sentence length just by a visual check.

This guideline should not come as a surprise. Nobody likes reading long sentences, given a choice – how about this one?

✖ The number of people who will be paying less is far greater than the

> number of people who will be paying more, but the amount extra being paid by the small number paying more is greater than the amount from the larger number who are paying less, and the two coming together come out to the same or near enough to the same revenue as before.
> *Sir Robert Muldoon*

How did you react as you grappled with that sentence, which has the outrageous EFLAW® score of 95? Did you stall at the first comma? Did you feel irritated, anxious or angry? Did you stop reading halfway through and start reading it a second time? If so, join the club. And you are, I guess, a native English speaker.

By the way, Sir Robert Muldoon's famous sentence uses no obscure words at all, and is grammatically correct.

Native English speakers have the option of simply reading faster, which helps us to comprehend a difficult passage. However, our international clients do not always have this choice. They're already reading as fast as they can. Their response to a difficult passage will be to read more slowly... and lose the thread completely. To empathise with them, try reading the original sentence by Muldoon very slowly, word by word. Notice how the passage seems even more obscure?

Long sentences can make people feel confused, disoriented and irritated. Can you blame them if they deposit the offending document in the Z file... forever?

Our aim is total clarity. Our international clients should not have to read any sentence twice to get the meaning. That means we must (surprise, surprise) write short sentences.

Why are long sentences such a problem?

I bet you've never heard anyone saying 'and eleventhly...'.

The limited capacity of our short-term memory is the critical factor. Think of words as items we have to hold in our head till we get to the end of the sentence.

In fact, an item for a native English speaker may be an entire phrase. Reading in our own language, we can stack up seven or eight phrases before our short-term memory becomes saturated. By contrast, in an unfamiliar language people tend to read word by word. In this case, the short-term memory can overflow very quickly.

Something similar happens when we write or speak a long sentence. As we add more and more words, we lose focus. That's why long sentences often contain grammar mistakes and muddled logic. That's why we sometimes panic in the middle of a long sentence, and cannot think how to finish it.

Below is a horror sentence for people from non-English-speaking backgrounds. It was in the Netscape 1.1 Handbook.

✖ If you want to send the current page as an attachment (this may be helpful if your recipient is going to reuse the document), choosing the **Document Text** item sends the text of the message intact (no > symbols are appended to each line) while choosing the **Document Source** item sends the text of the message embedded with all the HTML instructions that format Internet pages.

TRY THIS

Rewrite the passage below in Global English, using short sentences.

The Whitetown Community Interpreting Service Incorporated operates to provide access to interpreting services which ensures that all members of the community who are not native speakers of English are able to clearly understand information presented to them and that they are able to be understood.

Non-English-speaking consumers of your service are unable to achieve equal access to it unless they can communicate fully with your staff. They can, for example, be wrongly diagnosed, sign forms they did not understand, misunderstand instructions for further appointments or treatment or for their child's school or health needs.

Short sentences are always appropriate

Some people resist the idea of writing short sentences, and point to the 200-word sentences of writers like Janet Frame with admiration. But we're not writing literature, we're not aiming for elegance or originality. We are trying to convey information in English to people whose mother tongue is not English.

No matter what type of idea we are trying to communicate, we can do so very successfully in short sentences.

Complex ideas can be conveyed in short sentences

Many people tell me that their particular business cannot be conducted in simple English. They sincerely believe that complex information can be explained only in long, complex sentences. The opposite is true. The more complicated a concept, the greater the need to use short sentences when explaining it to an international audience.

Is there any business more complicated than neurobiology? Yet Daniel Alkon explains it most satisfactorily in language with a low EFLAW® score.

> *Within biological networks, signals travel between neurons along what are essentially telephone wires. The structure of each neuron extends into a long wirelike arm. When it reaches another neuron, the arm swells slightly into a small sack containing packets of chemical messages. Electrical signals spread from the main neuron along its arm to the sack, where the signals release the chemical messages onto the next neuron. In the next neuron, the new chemical signal triggers a new electrical signal, which releases still another chemical signal onto another neuron. In this way, a wave of signals spreads through a network of neurons carrying a processed image as it goes. As this wave passes from layer to layer, it moves along a pathway within the brain. You can think of the first group of neuron layers in this pathway as fulfilling the visualizing functions of a fancy camera.* Daniel L Alkon
>
> Average 18.25 words per sentence. EFLAW® score 23.87

Academic articles can be written in short sentences

Academic prose is almost inevitably loaded with abstract nouns, because the very subject may be abstract. But when sentences are short, abstract nouns cease to be a problem. Below, Tamae Prindle has made her theoretical paper internationally readable by using short sentences.

> *A segment of the ecofeminists argues that only the maternal instinct can save the earth from the patriarch's destructive modernisation. Others are fumbling for a de-gendered solution to ecological problems. Post-modern feminism transcends the gendered hierarchy as it honours the integrity of differences and similarities. Much of this Western development gained force in the 1970s, and the Japanese feminists followed in its wake.* Tamae Prindle
>
> Average 15.75 words per sentence. EFLAW® score 21.75

Passionate opinions can be conveyed in short sentences

I love reading letters to the editor from people who are feeling really hot under the collar. In the passion of the moment, their sentences often gallop off into the sunset, becoming more prolix and diffuse and attenuated and incoherent and convoluted and periphrastic (in other words, longer) as the emotion intensifies.

Raving successfully in short, clear sentences is an acquired skill. If sentences are short, there is some chance that international readers will understand the writer's point of view. An example follows.

The GDP (Gross Domestic Product) therefore is a crazy and destructive mismeasure of wellbeing. An oil tanker going aground adds to the GDP. The Cave Creek disaster was good for the economy. Divorce, production of nuclear armaments, lung cancer, car crashes, burglaries and muggings all add to growth. When we add up the goods and services in an economy, everything is shown as a credit. There are no debits in this outdated system. Our system of accounts is like a calculator that can add but not subtract. Deirdre Kent

Average 17 words per sentence. EFLAW® score 17.57

Profound ideas can be conveyed in short sentences

Your children are not your children. They are the sons and daughters of Life's longing for itself... .You can give them your love but not your thoughts, for they have their own thoughts... . You are the bows from which your children as living arrows are sent forth. Khalil Gibran

Average 11.5 words per sentence. EFLAW® score 16

Humour can be conveyed in short sentences

Guns aren't lawful;
Gas smells awful;
Nooses give;
You might as well live.
Dorothy Parker

13 words in the sentence. EFLAW® score 15

Attack long sentences with the axe

Scribere qui nescit, nullum putate esse laborem. (*People who don't know how to write think it is no trouble.*)

When you find you have written a longer sentence, you can often fix it by using the axe: simply chop the long sentence into two or three parts.

Then bind the wounds so that each sentence makes sense. To bind the wounds of a dismembered sentence, we can repunctuate, use a transition word or phrase, or change the structure.

Example

✖ While manufacturing changed from a one-shift to a two-shift operation, the top management decided to borrow the money to build a new factory.

First use the axe

While manufacturing changed from a one-shift to a two-shift operation, (**chop here!**) the top management decided to borrow the money to build a new factory.

Then bind the wound

✔ Manufacturing changed from a one-shift to a two-shift operation. Meanwhile (**transition word**), the top management decided to borrow the money to build a new factory.

Transition words and phrases are extremely useful in Global English. They help readers to follow our train of thought.

Examples of transition words and phrases

Firstly, Secondly, Thirdly, Also, Moreover, Finally, After this, Then, Consequently, Therefore, For this reason, This explains, Thus, As a result, Similarly, Likewise, For example, However, On the other hand, Nevertheless, Yet, In fact, Indeed, And, But, Otherwise

In the following passage, transition words and phrases are in bold.

Likewise, *the particles of the universe are not, by themselves, fundamental. An electron is no more fundamental than a neutrino. They appear to be fundamental only because our microscopes are not powerful enough to reveal their structure.* ***According to string theory****, if we could somehow magnify a point particle, we would actually see a small vibrating string.* ***In fact, according to this theory****, matter is nothing but the*

> *harmonies created by this vibrating string. Since there are an infinite number of harmonies that can be composed for the violin, there are an infinite number of forms of matter that can be constructed out of vibrating strings.* ***This explains*** *the richness of the particles in nature. Hyperspace.* Michio Kaku

Average 16.42 words per sentence. EFLAW® score 23.28

Starting sentences with And & But

It is grammatically correct to start a sentence with 'And' or 'But'. Most famous writers do, and every day we read such sentences. Placed at the beginning of a sentence, 'And' and 'But' function as transition words, easing the flow of one sentence to the next.

However, international clients generally expect rather formal English. Starting sentences with 'And' or 'But' is a useful sentence structure – but don't overuse it in Global English.

TRY THIS

Chop this sentence into three or four shorter sentences.

Payment in advance or open account trading is a common payment method with Australia, but by paying in advance you may not have seen the goods and you will not have yet received title to the goods by way of the transport documents.

Attack lists with bullets

> *Let there be light.*
> Genesis.1.3

Long sentences and solid blocks of English text create anxiety in many people from a non-English-speaking background. Solid text in Roman letters may seem dense, dark and dangerous.

Many long sentences contain lists. Often you can restructure a long sentence using bullet points. If used correctly, bullet points can reduce the reader's anxiety. They:

- break up frightening blocks of solid text
- isolate the points you make
- provide white space to rest the eye.

The proper role of bullet points is to draw attention to two, three or four short items in a list. A good example is the list above this paragraph.

Each bullet point in a group must be parallel in construction. They must all start with a similar word. Otherwise the list will be ambiguous.

Check that each item follows the stem perfectly. Does each line make sense? Does it sound right?

Example

Child-rearing is:

- difficult
- expensive
- satisfying.

Testing the list:

Child-rearing is difficult (does this sound right? ✔)

Child-rearing is expensive (does this sound right? ✔)

Child-rearing is satisfying (does this sound right? ✔)

Each bullet must come out of the same gun. Or to put it another way, think of the stem of a list as a socket. Each point you make must fit into that socket exactly. As with electrical equipment, the plug either matches the socket or it doesn't match. It cannot half match, or sort of match.

Even if you don't use bullets, a list must be correctly constructed. Here's an ungrammatical list within a sentence.

Example

Candidates, age 35 or over, will be fluent in English, Cantonese and Mandarin, possess a Computer Sciences degree and/or Business qualification and 7+ yrs similar experience within a multinational company.

Testing the list:

Candidates, age 35 or over, will be fluent in English, Cantonese and Mandarin (*does this sound right?* ✔)

Candidates, age 35 or over, will possess a Computer Sciences degree and/or Business qualification (*does this sound right?* ✔)

Candidates, age 35 or over, will 7+ yrs similar experience within a multinational company (*does this sound right*? ✖)

Typically, it's the last item that breaks the pattern.

Compress or subdivide long lists

While bullets are certainly excellent in Global English, don't put too many items on one list. Remember, our short-term memories have a limited capacity. Even native English speakers feel overwhelmed when too many bullet points appear together. For international readers, keep such lists to a maximum of six items.

Example of a bulleted list that is too long

✖ According to our interactive view of the reading process, any particular child may be attempting, with differing degrees of success, any of the following reading strategies:

- using meaning cues
- using structural cues
- using visual cues
- predicting on the basis of a cue or combination of cues
- checking on the basis of a cue or combination of cues
- re-reading to pick up more information
- re-reading to maintain meaning
- closely monitoring their reading
- reading with fluency
- reading with appropriate phrasing.

Ian Morrison. *Getting it Together. Reading theory and practice.*

One solution to the problem of a long list is to compress some of the bulleted points together.

✔ ...any particular child may be attempting any of the following reading strategies:

- using meaning cues, structural cues, or visual cues
- predicting or checking on the basis of one or more cues

- re-reading to acquire more information, or to maintain meaning
- monitoring their reading closely
- reading with fluency and appropriate phrasing.

Another solution is to subdivide the items (or use a table).

TRY THIS

Change the list below so that it is perfectly constructed.

According to *The Net* magazine (July 1995) the average users of the World Wide Web are:

- 25 to 55 years old
- have an average income of NZ$120 000 per annum
- 95% of users have four years or more tertiary education.

When brevity is not a virtue: the string of nouns

All through this book the same advice reverberates: be concise! But sometimes in the quest for brevity, we can get too enthusiastic. Then we may find ourselves writing strings of three or four nouns. These are not brief, but cryptic.This particular syndrome does not affect the EFLAWR score – but it certainly makes English harder for our international clients, and wastes their time.

The string of nouns often occurs in titles and names, and in technical jargon. It is a way of compressing a lot of information into a few words.

Examples

Refusal Review Authority

Application Management System

Income Support Service

Of course, we can't tinker with titles. But we must try to avoid using other strings of nouns, because they are often incomprehensible to international clients.

Examples

health care environment

electricity workers bribery scandal

branch exit assessment requirements

technology transfer decision tree

income protection liability implications

earthquake attenuation relationships

industry interface dialogue outcomes

Brevity is not a virtue if a phrase is incomprehensible. Strings of nouns must be rewritten so that they make sense to our international readers. Usually that means adding a few miniwords, so the new phrase is longer than the original. But provided the sentence is short, that's OK.

Example

✖ the provincial economy growth statistics

✔ growth statistics for the provincial economy

TRY THIS

Rewrite these strings of nouns to make them comprehensible to non-English speakers.

1 mountain bike trail improvement

2 check-out supervisors seminar

3 power company customers.

6

Use simple sentences

Do your best to be lucid. Simple sentences help.

The Economist Style Guide

Let me explain English word order in the crudest possible terms: in a classic English sentence, **somebody (or something) does (or is) something** – in that order. This pattern is our template for sentence construction in Global English. (In conventional terms, the classic English word order is Subject, Verb, Complement. In that order.)

The somebody-does-something pattern should be our default sentence structure. If we have something to add to the sentence, the extra words should usually go at the end.

In Global English, don't deviate from this simple sentence pattern unless you have a good reason. When you write to international clients, stick with the basic pattern until it bores you silly.

Why? Because people who speak a different language have a different word order imprinted on their brains. Word order varies greatly in other languages. For example, verbs are the last items in a German or Japanese sentence. Some languages don't even have a grammatical subject. Some languages put the object before the verb.

We can remove a lot of speed-bumps for our international clients if we structure sentences consistently, and resist the impulse to fiddle with the natural order of English.

Examples of the somebody-does-something sentence structure

A vaccine against cocaine (**something**) will help (**does**) drug users break the habit (**something**).

Malaysia (**somebody**) has debunked (**does**) Australia's efforts to be viewed as part of Asia (**something**).

The basic pattern may seem painfully obvious, yet the pattern is broken more often than it is followed, even in business English.

The trouble is, the voice of your English teacher is ringing in your ears. 'Don't start every sentence the same boring old way! Vary your sentences!'

When writing to international clients, dump that advice. Your English teacher probably graduated in English literature, and has a literary sort of English in mind. Subconsciously your teacher was always trying to teach you how to write a short story.

However, elegant prose is not required for our purpose. We are trying to communicate successfully with people with a different language background. They don't want to read fine sentences – they just want to know what we mean. Given a choice of clarity and elegance, we must choose clarity every time.

First things first

The great majority of men and women cannot appreciate literary style. If they do, they fear it.
Claude C. Hopkins

The beginning of every sentence is a prime site, so we mustn't dump rubbish on it. A good Global English sentence is founded on the first few words. Think of the beginning of a Global English sentence as a heading. Our first few words should tell the reader what the sentence is about.

We give our international readers confidence by putting the real subject very near the start. Here are three sentences that follow the rule:

✔ Both Washington and Tokyo denied the spying allegations and lodged protests with Beijing.

✔ Hong Kong soccer was thrown into chaos when senior clubs threatened to break away from the Hong Kong Football Association to form their own league.

✔ In 1995 the world produced a million tonnes of CFCs, the chemicals that do most of the damage to the ozone layer.

By contrast, read the sentence below. It is badly structured. It starts with a minor point, and the major point is buried at the end. Sentences with this sort of construction present difficulties for international readers. Note that the sentence is far too long for Global English. That figures: long sentences have a habit of spawning other problems.

✖ A related issue that stems from the culture of son preference and the inequality of the girl child is already manifest in rural China where, in some areas, there are 28 single men for every single woman.

Here's a better version of the sentence above.

✔ Men outnumber women in some areas of rural China by 28:1. The problem arises because the culture favours sons and discriminates against girl children.

TRY THIS

Shorten or chop up this sentence and rewrite it. Start with the real subject.

Western Business executives in Beijing said the only way for the SEZs to maintain their distinctiveness would be for them to offer something other parts of the country could not.

Don't start sentences with a meaningless word

The example below certainly follows the somebody-does-something pattern, but the 'somebody' is not the real subject of the sentence.

✖ You will find a notice in the hall advising you of the house rules.

By starting the sentence with a minor point, the writer is teasing and misleading international readers. The main point of the sentence is surely not that 'you will find a notice'. Two Global English versions of the sentence follow. Both are equally good, and both start with a real subject.

✔ A notice in the hall explains the house rules.

✔ The house rules are written on a notice in the hall.

For the same reason, be wary of starting sentences with 'it is' in Global English. This construction works occasionally, provided the sentence is short. But remember that the miniword 'it' presents problems for people who are not totally familiar with English.

Example

✖ It is still not clear whether paying holiday pay as part of employees' hourly rate is lawful, and it is safer not to do so.

In the sentence above, the word 'it' is meaningless. Here is the sentence rewritten in Global English, starting with a real subject.

✔ We cannot be certain that paying holiday pay as part of employees' hourly rate is lawful. Therefore, we recommend that you avoid this practice.

Another confusing way to start a sentence is 'there is' or 'there are'. Again, the first word ('there') has no meaning and is a false subject.

By the way, when a sentence starts with 'It is', 'There is' or 'There are', the sentence often runs out of control after about 15 words. Here is an example of a sentence running amok.

✖ There are many instances of people being very good at their profession but their business subsequently fails because they did not know how to prepare a full and realistic evaluation of the potential for their proposed business.

A better version of this sentence follows.

✔ Many businesses fail because the operators cannot evaluate their business's potential realistically. This type of business failure can occur even when the operators are very good at their profession.

TRY THIS

Rewrite the following sentences. Start each one with a real subject.

1 It is now 190 years since Roget first proposed his system of verbal classification.

2 There is indisputable evidence that one pair of rats can produce 100 000 descendants within three years

Put extra information last

Thus I got into my bones the essential structure of the ordinary British sentence – which is a noble thing.

Winston Churchill

A perfect Global English sentence flows smoothly, without interruption. All parts of the verb are together. The same applies to the subject and the object. Don't break the flow by adding extra information in mid-sentence. If you want to add some extra information, the best place is at the end of the sentence.

Example

✔ People (**somebody**) can understand (**does**) your writing (**something**) very easily (**extra information**).

✔ China and Algeria (**somebody**) have signed (**does**) an accord pledging co-operation on the peaceful use of nuclear technology (**something**), the official Xinhua news agency said yesterday (**extra information**).

The following sentence breaks the no-interruption rule in an exaggerated way – but deliberately, for rhetorical effect. It's certainly not a Global English sentence.

Now go and get a bucket and fill it with cold water and a bit of – wait for it... here it comes, the highly secret formula used by all discerning professional window cleaners... drum roll please – Dishwashing Liquid!

The sentences below disrupt the pattern for no good reason. Notice their nervous, zig-zag construction. This interrupted or erratic construction is a likely source of confusion for international clients.

✖ For many countries, an essential procedure before despatch is barcoding or product numbering of all products on the market.

✖ While economic reforms have prompted smaller enterprises to think of survival, bigger enterprises, when it comes to mergers and acquisitions, are still motivated by policy considerations.

Here are Global English versions of the same sentences. The new versions follow the somebody-does-something pattern, without interruption.

✔ Certain countries require you to barcode or number all the products you put on the market.

✔ Economic reforms have prompted smaller enterprises to focus on survival. Bigger enterprises are still motivated by policy when they consider mergers and acquisitions.

TRY THIS

Rewrite this sentence so that it follows the somebody-does-something pattern, without interruption.

Higher imports caused by reduced import duties and slower growth of exports overshadowed the earnings of foreign currencies.

One's enough, two's the limit, three's a disaster

One is one and two is two and ever more shall be so.

Green Grow the Rushes O!

Enough already! In Global English, one idea per sentence is sufficient. Sometimes a sentence can contain two ideas and still remain lucid. But as soon as we force three ideas into a sentence there's trouble. We are putting too great a strain on our international readers.

Many people think that unless they include every angle of a complicated idea in the same sentence, their readers will overlook some angles. Nothing could be more untrue. In fact, when a sentence contains three or more ideas, the sentence loses focus. Then most readers automatically forget some of the ideas, because they seem less important.

So if you are struggling to express a complex idea, break it down into single ideas in short sentences. Deconstruct it. Then your reader will regard each idea as important, and will have a good chance of following your argument.

The main idea in the following sentence is well and truly buried under a pile of other ideas.

✖ Perhaps it is my Irish heritage that causes me to shake my head in bewilderment at the large numbers of women in the West who voluntarily deprive themselves of food, while elsewhere in the world millions of women and men can only imagine the luxury of being able to choose not to eat.

Here's another twisty-twirly sentence. Which points of the argument survive in your memory after one reading? This isn't a test, by the way. It's not our fault if we can't understand this sentence – the fault is with the writer.

✖ This 'proto-industrialisation' featured low death rates (thanks to its rural setting, away from the urban guilds that had controlled manufacturing), high birth rates (thanks to the emergence of labour as families' only resource) and increasing working hours as cottagers competed against each other for contracts with the merchant employers who supplied their materials and bought their finished products.

As you see, trying to crush every detail of an idea into a single sentence is definitely counterproductive. The effect is one of mental constipation.

Our international clients should understand every sentence we write after one reading. That means that our sentences should contain one idea at best, two ideas at most.

The same applies when talking to a person or audience from a non-English-speaking background. We should separate our ideas into bite-sized pieces, and apply a mental full stop after every one.

Here are more sentences that contain too many ideas for your international clients to grasp. And how about you? Notice whether you really grasp the meaning on first reading.

✖ If ever modern Labour was less populist, less appealing, and, in real terms, in terms of effect rather than rhetoric, in terms of achieving goals through attaining power, if ever Labour actually offered less to women, it is hard to remember when.

✖ Perhaps no single idea is more deeply embedded in modern political culture than the belief that economic growth is the key to meeting most important human needs, including alleviating poverty and protecting the environment.

A Global English editor would chop up those sentences and reconstruct them using the simple somebody-does-something model. After discussion with the writer, they might emerge something like this.

✔ Modern Labour is at its lowest ebb as a populist party. It is less appealing and less effective than before. Labour's rhetoric does not convince voters. Labour is not achieving goals because it is not attaining power. And Labour offers less to women than ever before.

✔ One belief is deeply embedded in modern political culture. That is the belief that economic growth is the key to meeting most important human needs. Economic growth is even regarded as the key to alleviating poverty and protecting the environment.

TRY THIS

Rewrite the following text in short sentences, with only one idea in each sentence.

Perhaps the clearest example of a discipline where there seems to be nothing more to discover is geographical exploration – a possible exception being the deep ocean trenches.

Eliminate 'which' and 'that'

One type of sentence construction has great potential for causing international misunderstandings. **That** is sentences **that** include **'that'** or **'which'** or **'who'**, **which** are structures **that** people **who** write Global English should eliminate. (See what I mean?)

I'll show you what the problems are – but luckily, the solution is basically very simple. 'Which' and 'that' sentences cause so much trouble that whenever possible, just avoid them in Global English.

Native English speakers use 'which' and 'that' almost at random, unaware of any rules. Some international clients have learned the correct – though obsolete – grammar rules. This complicates matters.

The first problem: 'which' and 'that' inevitably make sentences longer.

✖ The presence of dust mites, which are abundant in Hong Kong because of the atmosphere, would be studied because they had been found to affect 90% of asthmatics.

The following edited version is much easier to understand:

✔ Dust mites are abundant in Hong Kong because of the atmosphere. Dust mites will be studied because they affect 90% of asthmatics.

The second problem: commas change the meaning.

The travellers, who were **from Singapore**, were delayed two hours.

The travellers **who were from Singapore** were delayed two hours.

The above two sentences have completely different meanings. Can we be sure our international reader will know the difference? Here's one way of rewriting without using 'who', 'which' or 'that'.

✔ The travellers **from Singapore** were delayed two hours.

The third problem: according to some pernickety grammarians, the meaning of the sentence changes according to whether you use 'which' or 'that'.

The planes **that** were from Korea were delayed (*i.e. all the planes*).

The planes **which** were from Korea were delayed (*i.e. only the planes from Korea*).

Never mind this often-broken rule – just take the easy way out. Say what you mean another way, avoiding both 'which' and 'that'.

✔ The planes from **Korea** were delayed.

✔ The planes were delayed on their way from Korea.

One more problem: 'which' and 'that' clauses often interrupt a thought.

✖ The city needs billions of dollars to satisfy energy needs and, because energy development is a priority under the Ninth Five-Year Plan, which starts next year, Shenergy should receive support.

As so often, the best solution is to use the axe and chop the sentence into two or more.

✔ The city needs billions of dollars to satisfy its energy needs. Energy development is a priority under the Ninth Five-Year Plan, starting next year. Therefore Shenergy will probably receive support.

Now you understand all the problems of 'which' and 'that'...

Do you really need these troublesome words in your Global English documents? Answer: no, you can communicate without them.

It's OK to use an occasional 'which' or 'that' if the whole sentence is short. But be aware that as soon as you introduce the words 'which' or 'that', you are gambling with clarity.

TRY THIS

Rewrite this sentence in Global English. Don't use 'which' or 'that'. Have no qualms about repeating key words: this practice is highly recommended.

He said he would also ask the National People's Congress, to which he is a delegate, to investigate.

7

Negatives are a no-no

Yes, we have no bananas!

Any course on writing normal business English insists on positive language, and rightly so. Negative language has the power to confuse even native English speakers. When communicating with international clients, the same advice applies tenfold.

People find it hard to visualise things that do not exist. We find it hard to visualise something in terms of what it is not. (Leo Tolstoy and his brother believed anything they wished would come true – if they could stand in a corner and not think of a white bear for ten minutes.) Different cultures meet the challenge of expressing negative thoughts in entirely different ways.

For example, in English, the mathematical principle applies: two negatives cancel each other out and create a positive. In correct English usage, not improbable implies probable. Yet in Spanish, a double negative is a negative with knobs on. The Spanish equivalent of not improbable means very probable.

So people from non-English-speaking backgrounds prefer positive English firstly for linguistic reasons.

- Their own language may have no equivalent of some English negative structures.
- Negative English may be impossible to translate.
- A negative sentence translated literally may mean the exact opposite of what was intended.

Cultural factors are very significant. In some cultures, saying negative things is regarded as tactless or even aggressive.

Then there are psychological factors. Generally, a positive message creates less anxiety than a negative message. Our international clients are likely to feel anxious when operating in a language that isn't their mother tongue. Our aim is to make them feel less anxious, so positive language is best.

Obvious negative expressions are the easiest to spot. But we frequently use partial negatives, or quasi-negatives – expressions that subtly imply a negative.

✖ Your application will be processed only if you send the prerequisite forms.

The above sentence has a hidden negative implication. A few simple changes transforms it into a positive, easily understood statement.

✔ Your application will be processed after we receive the prerequisite forms.

Signs of negative language and hidden negatives

negative words	negative prefixes and suffixes
no not won't never nowhere nothing nobody	un- de- dis- non- in- contra- counter- anti- -less
negative implications	
remove unfortunately mistake unless only if despite	however until default remove cancel except

Negative language, negative effects

Negative language can create a tone that is old-fashioned, peevish, pedantic, cynical and depressing. An extreme example of negative writing is found in the historical novel *House of Strife*. Author Maurice Shadbolt uses negative language to show the character of his hero, and to convey a nineteenth century atmosphere.

> *The first time I saw John Heke he was no disappointment... Huntsman Heke appeared to take no joy in his bloody trophies. When he sighted me he mustered no pretence of pleasure either.... He said nothing.... Finally his eyes found a place of rest forward of his horse. At no point did they meet mine.*
>
> *I have not been looking for you,' he disclosed.... It was not a stirring encounter. It would be better unremembered.*
>
> Maurice Shadbolt

Remember Pollyanna and her glad game? Even in a pit full of scorpions she would find something to be glad about. We should all try to play the glad game in international communications. When our business is global, positive language can win business and prevent misunderstandings. Practice makes perfect, fortunately.

If we are obliged to say something negative to an Asian person, it is preferable to deliver the bad news face to face if possible.

Examples

✖ There is no reason for New Zealand to replicate Australia's constitutional wrangle no more than we should adopt its outdated industrial-relations practice.

A positive version of the sentence:

✔ New Zealand should go its own way. New Zealand can avoid a constitutional wrangle like Australia's. New Zealand's industrial-relations practice is more modern than Australia's.

TRY THIS

Rewrite the following sentence in Global English, using positive language.

Mr Lowe's tally of 156 competing commercial radio stations was extraordinary, but not exhaustive of all competition for radio companies.

Not only... but also...

One deadly kind of negative sentence is the 'Not only... but also...' sentence.

Example

✖ Not only is he not to blame, but he is not responsible either. Excusing himself, he said he was not told by his officials there were systemic defects.

✔ Mr Smith said he was innocent, and his officials were responsible for the breakdown. Mr Smith explained that only his officials were aware of the systemic defects.

How on earth can we fix the next sentence with its quadruple negative? The trouble is that the writer is trying to be witty.

✖ Not only do at least a third of all sitting MPs not know whether they will be back after the next election, but they don't know which party they might not be back for.

Wit, sarcasm, irony and jokes are all lost on people from a non-English-speaking background. The cultural context that makes us laugh at our own jokes is simply not there. All attempts at humour will probably be taken literally and cause confusion or worse. Here's a better version.

✔ At least a third of all sitting MPs know that they might lose their seats in the next election. Moreover, some of them are likely to change parties before the election or soon after.

Negative questions are dynamite

Please use a non-empty search string.

For our international clients, questions in the negative are fiendishly difficult. In many languages, the logical answer is 'yes' when an English speaker would answer 'no'.

✖ Question:	'Aren't you busy?'
International client:	'Yes.'
'Yes' means:	'You are right: I am not busy.'

A great many languages differ from English in the way they answer negative questions. For example, in French, 'si' is a special version of 'yes', reserved for contradicting a person who asks a negative question. In Japan, saying 'no' is a difficult undertaking.

Many Asian readers simply cannot answer negative questions in English: the chasm between the two languages and cultures is too great.

✖ Question: 'The temperature is rising, isn't it?'

International client: (silence)

Silence means: 'What do you mean? I can't reply.'

We can solve this problem by phrasing all questions and instructions in a positive way.

Read the sentence below, intended for new members of the Chamber of Commerce. It is quite unnecessarily phrased in a negative way. Can you understand it after just one reading? Would you check the Yes box or the No box?

✖ Please tick here if you do not wish us to pass on your name for direct marketing promotions from other companies.

The following item occurs quite often on the Internet. Do you hesitate before deciding whether to click or not? I hesitate!

✖ Hate saving time and money? Don't click here.

In New Zealand's 1993 parliamentary elections, ethnic voters were asked to complete the form below. Notice that each question has two parts. They are therefore impossible to answer with a simple 'Yes' or 'No'. In Global English, write questions with only one part.

✖ I am a New Zealand citizen but I have not been in New Zealand at all during the last three years. Yes No

I am a permanent resident of New Zealand but I have not been in New Zealand at all during the last year. Yes No

A Global English version would have been simplified like this:

✔ I am a New Zealand citizen Yes No

I am a permanent resident of New Zealand Yes No

I have been out of New Zealand continuously for the last three years. Yes No

TRY THIS

Rewrite the following in a positive way.

1 Is your company uninsured? If so, do not hesitate to contact one of our agents.

2 Do you agree that the number of professional firemen should not fall below the number employed nationally as at 31 January 1996?

Watch for hidden negatives in letters you receive from Asia

Although Japan presents the clearest example, negative expressions in Asia-Pacific communications are generally unwelcome. Therefore, when writing to an Asia-Pacific colleague, put yourself in a positive frame of mind and think of ways that you can express your thoughts positively.

David L. James

Difficulties with 'yes' and 'no' are also important in reverse. When you receive documents from Asia, particularly, be aware of hidden negatives and confusion over 'yes' and 'no'.

Some Asian cultures regard 'no' as a rude word. So they soften a refusal by referring to it vaguely. To add to the problem, they may say 'yes'. 'Yes' in Japan often means 'I understand what you are suggesting' – not 'yes, I agree to your terms'. Many a negotiator (including President Clinton) has been fooled by this custom.

Example

We thought your suggested improvements were very interesting. It will be a little difficult to implement them.

To say something is 'a little difficult' is a classic Japanese way of saying it won't happen. The speaker expresses refusal indirectly to preserve harmony and protect the other person from embarrassment.

TRY THIS

What does 'yes' mean in the following text?

'The infrastructure of Kobe is not yet fully restored, is it?' 'Yes.'

TRY THIS

Rewrite the following passage in positive language.

Taiwanese teachers said they saw no cultural barriers to using any of the books from the Kidbook series. The Babybook series did not get such a strong positive response.

8

Order, order!

Far too many relied on the classic formula of a beginning, a muddle and an end.

Philip Larkin

When an international client picks up a document we have sent, a certain anxiety prevails. Whether relatively fluent in English or a beginner, our client is worrying about two things: 'What's this document about?' And 'Am I going to be able to understand it?'

To a person from a non-English-speaking background, any document in the English language is like a foreign country – and it's our country, we are the host. We can leave our readers floundering in the undergrowth, and await the inevitable misunderstandings and delays. Or we can choose to guide readers through the document. Structure is the key.

Weak structure confuses international readers. If our structure is weak, they may become disoriented, miss the main point or misunderstand the significance of a point. If we use a strong structure the international reader is far more likely to read, react and respond.

Different cultures structure their documents in different ways. Americans favour getting straight to the point. Russians are said to be even more blunt. Some Asian cultures favour gentle allusion and a lateral approach to structure.

To guide international readers through a document, the following structural tricks will help.

- Provide a list of contents and if necessary a glossary.
- Number all paragraphs.

- Organise the contents according to a strict plan.
- Use clear headings, subheadings and key words.
- Repeat key words.

Structure is supremely important when giving speeches and presentations to international clients. The next chapter gives advice on structuring speeches for an international audience.

Provide a list of contents and a glossary

Any international document longer than four or five pages should have a list of contents. For your clients, this is obviously a godsend: they now have a map of your document. They can see where they're going. This creates confidence.

And strangely, writing a list of contents also helps us to structure a document properly. When we make a list of contents we can't help thinking about the order of the various items. If the order seems illogical, we can then fix it.

A glossary also provides relief for international clients. Think about the terms used in your document. Will your reader know what they mean? Are those terms used in exactly the same way in both cultures? If there's any doubt, we can either explain them in the text, or provide a glossary of all the doubtful words with their meanings.

TRY THIS

> List three words that you would need to explain or define in a document to be sent abroad. Give their meanings in Global English.

Number the paragraphs

One, two, three,
Mother caught a flea,
Put it in the teapot
And made a cup of tea.

Nursery Rhyme

Numbering the paragraphs is like providing street numbers for the items in a document.

You're going to love using this brilliant and simple device. And when an international client begins a discussion about some point you made, you will send me roses and chocolates and Lamborghinis.

That's how grateful you'll be for this simple tip.

When writing longer documents for international clients, I suggest you give every paragraph a number. I don't mean the conventional 1.1.1, 1.1.2 system of numbering. I mean consecutive numbers: 1, 2, 3, 4... and so forth until you reach the end. (In a letter, you can leave the courtesy paragraphs unnumbered, but number every paragraph about business.)

If you've never numbered paragraphs before, try it soon. You'll find that it can make an enormous difference to subsequent communication. When your client responds to the document, you can both simply refer to 'paragraph 29', for example. Discussion can begin immediately, without laborious repetition or paraphrase.

A lucky spinoff is that numbering paragraphs improves our writing. When we are conscious that every paragraph will be numbered, we're much more likely to confine ourselves to one topic per paragraph – and that's important in Global English.

Numbering paragraphs is dead easy with a computer. With a few clicks, every paragraph in a long document can be numbered.

Organise the contents according to a plan

Organising the contents of a document is like creating a good road system, with clearly marked highways and minor roads. A good, strong structure helps non-English-speaking readers to follow our thoughts, decide whether to read on, and choose what to read next.

What information should go first in a document? What goes last? What is the most important point? How much detail is needed? What goes in and what goes out? How long should the document be? How long should the various parts be?

These are all structural decisions. Try to make them early in the writing process. Then rewriting will be kept to a minimum.

If we don't consciously structure our writing, it probably has an illogical or chaotic structure.Then our confused and disoriented reader must stumble around in the dark, trying to find our main point.

Structure is a little tricky because thoughts begin in the brain, which is three-dimensional. In the brain, ideas rush along many paths simultaneously, they explode and high-jump and divaricate at phenomenal speed. Thinking is a three-dimensional activity. When we convert our thoughts into print or speech, we have to squeeze them into a two-dimensional queue. To write or speak involves imposing a ruthless structure on our teeming thoughts.

Maybe you have never consciously thought about questions of structure. When addressing other English-speaking people, we can often fluke successful communication. But for international communication, the intuitive approach to structure just won't do.

We can use structure as a powerful tool for international communication – and it's easy when you know how.

Put the most important item first

A recurring rule of thumb for Global English is 'first things first'. This structure helps international readers to follow our train of thought. It's simple, because the same rule applies to the sentence, the paragraph, and the entire document:

- put the real subject of a sentence first in every sentence (see Chapter Six)
- start every document with the most important point, or with a summary of the whole
- start every paragraph with a topic sentence.

Start longer documents with a summary of the document

Any international document should start with a sort of *Reader's Digest* version of the whole. This is the executive summary, and it's ten times as important when your reader is not a native English speaker.

For international readers, the summary of even a *War and Peace*-sized document should be very short – one page is perfect, two pages is usually too long. At all costs, write the summary in Global English. This enables readers with varying English ability to grasp the main points, and to discuss them.

Use the inverted triangle structure for international documents

Most business writing in English is structured as an inverted triangle: the 'biggest' or most important point comes first, usually in a subject line or the first sentence. Minor points follow, in order of decreasing importance.

The classic inverted triangle structure is excellent for most proposals, speeches and reports in Global English. The main difference is that when writing to international clients you should be ten times more strict. If you're good at structuring documents for consumption in New Zealand, England or the USA, then all you have to do when structuring Global English is to try even harder.

Everybody tends to put difficult documents aside for later... or forever. The first paragraph in your document may be the only part your international clients try to read. So make sure the first item is the one thing that your readers need to know.

When deciding what the most important point of your document is, remember to put yourself in the shoes of your readers. What is the most important point to them? That should be the first item they encounter.

To your Asian clients, the most important thing is probably their relationship with you. Therefore in a letter or fax, the first paragraph should strengthen that relationship. (See Chapter 11.)

Structure of proposals and reports

Longer proposals, reports and other impersonal documents should also follow the 'first things first' principle. If we bury the main point of our proposal deep in the text, it may never be read by our international readers.

1 Title page
2 Table of contents
3 Glossary
4 Summary of entire document
5 Most important points
6 Less important points.

As with normal business English, there are some exceptions to this rule – for example, when your purpose is to persuade. But whenever you have an urge to diverge from the rule, think very carefully first. Messing with the classic structure may sink your message in concrete boots.

Structure of Global English letters and faxes

For Global English letters, add a courtesy paragraph at the beginning and end. Make the middle section crystal clear. The following pattern is an excellent blueprint.

1 Subject line (unless the subject is very sensitive)
2 Courtesy paragraph

3 Most important point
4 What happens next
5 Explanation and/or less important points
6 Courtesy paragraph.

Apart from the subject line, this is exactly the same structure as my children used to use when they burst into the house after school.

1 Courtesy paragraph: 'Mummy! Mummy! Where are you?'
2 Most important point: 'Our class is going on a school trip!'
3 What happens next: 'You have to sign this form.'
4 Explanation and less important points: 'We're going to Castlepoint at Easter time and we have to have nametags on all our clothes and a sleeping bag and a torch and a waterproof coat, and Janie can't go because her grandmother is coming over from Singapore for a family reunion I'm going to share a tent with Andrea and Maria and Tracey.'
5 Courtesy paragraph: 'Oh! You've got your best dress on. Are we going out?'

TRY THIS

Restructure the letter below so that it is appropriate to send to an international client. Add anything you think is necessary.

Dear Sir or Madam

Contaminated ice-cream

Some contamination has been found in Batch #NP856 of vanilla ice-cream. Please check your shelves. If you have any products from this batch number, please destroy them. When you contact us with details, we will refund your money in full.

Yours sincerely

Michael Angelo

Start every paragraph with a topic sentence

A Global English paragraph must be about just one thought or topic. When the topic changes, start a new paragraph. It's that simple.

Every paragraph should begin with a topic sentence. Always! (The topic sentence tells what the paragraph is about.)

A consistent structure is marvellously reassuring for our international clients. When they realise that the main point will always come first in any paragraph, they can relax and concentrate on the meaning. A state of trust is established. Everything's under control, and they can keep on touring through your document.

Examples

In the following short paragraphs, the topic sentences are printed in bold.

✔ **As a yoga teacher, I am also interested in the performance of the body on different foods.** I have found that a simple, light diet, centred around fresh and lightly-cooked vegetables and fruit, has a dramatic effect on the body. Energy increases, joints move freely and muscles relax.

✔ **Use only a light pressure on the glass, and think fluid strokes.** You're not scraping paint, you're dancing on a film of foam, like Torvill and Dean.

TRY THIS

Write a short topic sentence for the following paragraph.

I needed to take control of my life. It seemed so silly clutching a packet of cigarettes every time I went anywhere. I ate my way through vast quantities of apples, and put aside my 'cigarette money' and paid off a motor bike. Since then I have bought a carpet, foodmixer, sewing machine and microwave oven. I take my pocket money to the value of the cigarettes my husband buys.

Use frequent explanatory headings in Global English

A heading saying 'Introduction' is about as useful as a roadsign saying 'USA'.

We can steer international readers through a document by adding explanatory headings and subheadings. These are like clear, accurate signposts.

Example

In the following example, the heading summarises what is in the following paragraph. It is not merely a neutral phrase: it suggests the writer's attitude or opinion.

Introductions are important

They are worth your time, thought and effort. Half the battle is won when you hook your audience and grab its attention with your introduction.

Explanatory headings tell readers what to expect

Think of headings as newspaper headlines that explain or summarise the articles below. A good Global English heading tells the reader exactly what to expect in the following text.

For a person from a non-English-speaking background, an explanatory heading is much more useful than a label.

✔ Explanatory Headings (useful)	✖ Labels (less useful)
Introductions are important	Introductions
Boy cycle racer	Sports event
Directing the meeting	Meeting procedure
Select your personalised listing format	Listing
Webodex organises the Net	New Net software

The best headings are not vague or neutral. They usually suggest an action, an event or a point of view.

Cute or clever-clever headings may impress native English speakers, but most international clients will be completely mystified by them. If you write teaser headings – say goodbye to your international readers.

Examples

Below are examples of headings that would be incomprehensible to most international readers.

- ✖ Fairness, fouls and foul-ups
- ✖ Dirty diggers unite
- ✖ Yours pompously
- ✖ Binary bulimia.

How many headings does Global English need?

Plenty! International readers should never be far from a heading. They should always be able to see at least one heading or subheading. Then they will never get lost in our prose.

This means we should usually use:

- at least two headings or subheadings on every A4 page
- on the Internet, at least two headings per screen.

TRY THIS

Write an explanatory heading for the following paragraph.

Abraham Lincoln stood absolutely still, straight, and quiet. He never touched the podium, made wild gestures, or walked around. On the other hand, Theodore Roosevelt was a fiery, vital, and bombastic speaker who used his whole body as an instrument of expression.

Repeat key words in Global English

Key words are another useful type of signpost to keep international readers on track. Remember, repetition is a virtue in Global English. It's best to keep using the same word for the same thing, without variation.

Please don't try to be 'literary', like this:

✖ Last week's **seminar** on Global English was oversubscribed. The **workshop** will be repeated on 5 June to accommodate those who could not attend. If you would like to attend the next Global English **presentation**, please contact LEARNZ Ltd on telephone (04) 384 7106.

Reading the paragraph above, international readers may assume there are three different events: a seminar, a workshop and a presentation. In a case like this, choose the best word, and stick with it throughout the document.

Here is a Global English version of the same paragraph.

✔ Last week's **seminar** on Global English was oversubscribed. The **seminar** will be repeated next month to accommodate those who could not attend. If you would like to attend the next Global English **seminar**, please contact LEARNZ Ltd on telephone (04) 384 7106.

TRY THIS

Rewrite the paragraph below. Use the same word for the same thing. Use bullet points if you like.

We have compared the **benefits** of e-mail with the **advantages** of the fax. There are three **problems** with faxes. The first **difficulty** is cost. The second **headache** is thermal paper. The third **complication** is size.

9

Speaking to international audiences

Have something to say, and say it as clearly as you can.
Matthew Arnold

So far, this book has concentrated largely on written communication. How about speaking to foreigners? The following sobering quotation comes from Patricia L. Kurtz, a language and communications consultant with years of international experience.

> *The privileged position of English in international discourse has allowed us to be unconscious of the difficulties many non-native English speakers encounter when we speak. Too many of us wing our way through international communication situations on automatic pilot. We speak too fast. We fling idiomatic phrases at our listeners. We concoct complicated sentences. We indulge in aimless digressions that frustrate and confuse. We imprecisely pronounce some of our words and swallow others. We just assume we will be understood.*
>
> *This behaviour sometimes impresses our international colleagues as arrogance.*
>
> Patricia L. Kurtz.

Is it arrogance? Or simply ignorance? Learning a few good habits can prevent us from seeming arrogant when we address an international audience.

Some people get quite tense at the prospect of talking to adults from a non-English-speaking culture. Maybe it's fear of the unknown. 'Will these people understand what I am saying? Will I understand what they are saying? Will we make progress in our discussions?'

How do you feel about talking to Asian people, for example? Nervous? Relaxed? Impatient? Judging how to speak can be quite confusing. Many people subconsciously equate intelligence with impeccable English; this error can certainly make us seem condescending, especially when dealing with people who speak two or three languages.

To communicate successfully, goodwill is the main ingredient. If we respect the other person and really want to communicate, it will surely happen, one way or the other. We can build on that respect with the skills and aids discussed in this chapter. And relax! Tension is definitely counter-productive.

An international audience is strongly influenced by the way we use our voice and the way we move and behave. When we communicate orally, our non-verbal messages speak louder than words: some experts claim that words account for only seven per cent of what we convey! A little retraining of our voice and body is essential, and can hugely improve the impression we make.

How to talk to international clients

Speak slowly

Yes, first and foremost, speak slowly! It's hard to judge your own speed without feedback. First, start talking so slowly that you can hardly bear it. And then ask your audience (slowly), 'Am I speaking too fast?' They will surely say you are.

Our talking apparatus is in top gear most of the time. When we first try to speak slowly, we probably change down to third gear, and imagine we are delaying traffic for miles behind. But in many situations, we need to change down to second or even first gear. Relax! More haste, less speed.

It's essential to talk naturally (using notes if appropriate). Never simply read a written speech, because you'll inevitably read too fast for an international audience. When we talk, it's much, much easier to slow down and to repeat things.

Pauses help to slow the pace. / / Pause often. / / Exaggerate pauses. / / Deliberately pause after every sentence, every headline, and every new topic. / / This is quite easy to do.

Enunciate clearly

Speak like a written page. Enunciate consonants in the middle of a word. Enunciate the final letters of words. Separate each word from the others: don't run them together. Say / one / word / then / say / the / next.

The reason for this advice is that people in non-English-speaking countries can often read English comparatively well. (They have more opportunities to read English than to hear it.) Thesoundsofourvoices areveryunlikethesamewordsonthewrittenpage. If we enunciate clearly, and separate our words, the audience finds it easier to recognise them.

Remember that international listeners must often strain to understand our accent. They need a little time to tune in. Perhaps their English teacher had a Californian accent. If so, an Oxford accent is a major challenge – and vice versa. Heavens, I remember once sitting in utter bewilderment at a conference in Cincinnati. To my amazement, I couldn't understand a single word, even though everyone was speaking English. As a New Zealander fresh from home, I took a full five minutes to tune into the babel of American accents around me.

DON'T SHOUT!!!!!!

Shouting is an instinctive reaction by some people when they feel they are not being 'heard'. Shouting will make matters worse. Shouting is boorish at best, and may have unknown cultural implications – for example, it may indicate you are losing control. (In some cultures people speak very softly when they want to control a meeting or a class.)

Notice the level of the voices of your hosts at the meeting or conference, and try to match that. Read the faces of the people furthest away from you; their expressions will reveal whether they can hear you.

TRY THIS

Read the following passage aloud, as if to an international audience. Speak slowly, enunciate every consonant, and say each word separately. Practise speaking this way until it sounds natural to you.

If you are the guest or the junior person, you should begin the procedure of exchanging business cards immediately after you are greeted. Present your business card with both hands. Make sure

continued...

the business card is the right way up, so that the script faces the other person. When you receive a business card, read it carefully, and comment on it. At a business meeting, place the cards on the table in front of you. For easy reference, arrange cards in the positions that people are seated. Treat business cards with great respect, because they represent the person in an almost spiritual way. Keep them in a special card case in your top pocket if you are a man, or in your handbag if you are a woman.

Adapt your non-verbal communication

In any country except our own we are the foreigners. We are likely to make blunders of etiquette at every turn. When in Japan I feel like the clumsiest, most ignorant oaf on earth, doing the wrong thing 90 times a day with every possible part of my anatomy. I am sometimes gently corrected, but usually forgiven (I think).

I'm sure that too many people have warned you about the cultural traps of international communication. Don't panic! People in every country are surprisingly tolerant provided we show goodwill and some effort to learn. It's OK to make mistakes.

Here are a few hints.

- Study the culture before you go abroad.
- For etiquette and body language, watch your hosts carefully and take your cue from them.
- In Asia, don't expect or try to close a deal on your first trip.
- Expect to be constantly astonished – and to enjoy yourself!

Be sensitive about eye contact

In a group situation, observe speakers from the host culture. How long do their eyes maintain contact with you? Take your cue from them.

With European people we get brownie points for our ability to maintain eye contact. A good way is to meet the eyes of many individual people in different parts of the room. In a small meeting, look at everybody in turn. Eye contact gives us useful feedback about how successfully we are communicating.

If your audience is Asian, it is often a good idea to sweep your eyes smoothly over the entire audience at the start and end of your speech. Include everybody. The audience wishes to be 'seen' as a group. Try looking at people using a soft focus, or look just above their heads.

In Asia, don't despair if you see people with their eyes shut. They may not actually be nodding off. They may just be concentrating hard on what you are saying – that's their story, anyway! If you want them to open their eyes, show some visual aids.

In an Asian group, try not to single out individuals and eyeball them. Sustained eye contact may make those individuals – and others – uncomfortable. Glance at many different people each for a brief time only.

But don't worry if this generalised, inclusive eye contact is too difficult to sustain – just do your best. People will expect you to behave like an English-speaking person, and will make allowances.

Body language

When a native English speaker meets a non-English speaker, each is wondering how to behave. Ideally, each is trying to meet the other person halfway. So we do have a certain latitude in our attempts to behave appropriately. We just need to do our homework, keep alert for hints and signals, and do our best.

We can't go far wrong if we behave formally with international clients and colleagues. Be reserved, calm, correct and polite, particularly in Asia. It takes time and energy to become friends. Later, the formality may ease off in certain situations – but it's unwise to initiate that relaxation. We should always take our cue from the host.

Eliminate bad habits

Are you a swayer, a rocker, a twitcher, a sloucher, a joker, a foot-tapper, a money-jiggler, an eye-popper, or a head-wobbler?

OK, we all have some funny habits. But in a non-English-speaking environment, these habits can be really distracting and damaging. Your audience is trying to listen and to think in English, which is a very demanding process. Moreover, you want to gain their respect as a person of some dignity.

In every culture some body language is offensive. Do you fling your arms and legs around? Do you point your finger at people? Do you blow your nose in public? Do you slap people on the back? Do you fake anger as a rhetorical device? All these habits signify something bad in at least one other culture – perhaps impatience, insolence, brashness, aggression, vulgarity, childishness or a shameful loss of control.

Learn to give presentations the safe way: be still and be calm.

If you have any brutally frank colleagues, ask them for feedback. Even more effective, make a video of yourself in action. Try very hard to eliminate the bad habits that mask the true and beautiful inner you, before you take a business trip abroad.

And by the way, when in Asia, don't treat handshakes as a contest of strength. People in Asia may expect to shake your hand, because you are a Westerner. Most prefer a very brief and gentle clasp. Occasionally someone will try to shake your hand the Western way and leave you bruised and trembling. A slight bow (very slight!) is perfectly acceptable – and safe.

Use Global English

You're well prepared by now to choose the right language for speaking to international clients. Just use Global English, and all will be well.

- Use very short, very simple sentences.
- Use words with only one meaning.
- Repeat the same key words for the same things.
- Ask only simple, positive questions.
- Say who is doing what (beware of pronouns).
- Never tell jokes or use slang.
- Avoid phrasal verbs.
- Avoid or explain idioms and metaphors.

Repeat yourself whenever necessary. That might be rather often. Read the faces of your audience for signs of bewilderment, and say it again – and later, again.

If you don't understand something, paraphrase or repeat to check the meaning:

'Do you mean...?'

'Do I understand this correctly? ....'

'I think you said.... Is that correct?'

These are useful phrases too:

'I'd like to know more about that.'

'Would you repeat that, please?'

Avoid negative expressions like 'I can't understand you' or 'you're not clear'. It's bad manners to imply that the speaker's English is poor.

Speeches and presentations

For the cross-lingual audience, it is best to limit the key points to three or four... . Making deep grooves on a few essential points is preferable to briskly skating over too many.

Patricia L. Kurtz

Structure speeches rigidly

When preparing speeches or presentations for an international audience, our most significant aid to successful communication is probably structure. The structure of an international speech should be ruthlessly symmetrical and predictable. No diversions, no impulsive asides, no amusing irrelevancies. Just a carefully plotted speech, making a limited number of strongly connected points. Four key points is enough.

You know how it is when you listen to a speech. You drift in and out even at the best of times. This is perfectly natural – in fact, it is physiologically inevitable. An international audience will certainly be doing the same thing: their attention will be flickering on and off. Unlike us, they need very large hooks and signposts to draw them back into the speaker's train of thought.

The greatest risk is that some listeners will get lost early in our speech, and never return to the fold. When they drift away for a moment (and they will) they may lose not just the odd sentence, but the entire context. We can retain or regain their attention by:

- choosing key words and repeating them throughout
- emphasising structure by repeating phrases like 'The first effect of ... is....' 'The second effect of ... is....'
- providing a short outline of our speech on paper
- using visual aids.

The following guidelines will help you prepare your speech. Not much room to move, is there? To structure a speech for an international audience, I suggest staying within these strict limits.

Topic
Key words
Key point 1
Key point 2
Key point 3
Key point 4

TRY THIS

Using the guidelines above, prepare for a presentation or speech you might give to a non-English-speaking audience. Limit yourself to six phrases.

Provide a short outline in advance

Prepare a very short, very simple outline of your speech. Use headings and key words. Use extremely short sentences, no longer than this one. Print the outline with plenty of white space, and make the headings (and therefore the structure) very obvious. Number your points 1, 2, 3, 4, 5.... You can quote these numbers in your speech to keep your audience on track.

This outline must be extremely short. One page is almost too long. The audience should be able to read the summary swiftly before the speech begins.

To give the audience a full version of a speech in advance is to sabotage the occasion. All we will see as we deliver our presentation is an array of hair and bald pates, as the audience reads on... and on... and on.... The full text and any other explanatory material can be distributed after we have spoken.

TRY THIS

Prepare a half-page outline of a speech you might make to an international audience. Choose any topic.

Supplement the speech with visual aids

The meaning of the communication is the response you get.
Joseph O'Connor and John Seymour

Good visual aids quadruple our chances of being understood by an international audience. Don't even think about giving a speech in an international environment without some appropriate visual aids.

No matter how carefully we research, we can never be sure just how good our audience's English will be. An international audience of 50 might consist of 49 people with degrees from Harvard or Cambridge, plus one whose English consists of 'Hello!' Or the other way round. Or any other combination.

For this reason, always assume that some people in your audience will be unable to figure out what you are saying. Support your words with plenty of visual aids. Of course, check your hosts' technology before leaving home.

Slides and transparencies can be wonderfully effective. Overhead projectors are commonly used even in developing countries.

These are visual aids, so make them graphic. Use charts, tables, graphs, photographs, maps and line drawings. Any figures should be shown in the context of charts or graphs, because written numbers are problematical in an international context. (Different cultures write numbers in different ways.) Convert financial figures into local currency. Provide short, simple captions in Global English for all slides and overhead transparencies.

It's OK to show simple phrases and key words, but any verbal slides should be super-simple – maybe four or five words at most. Full sentences on slides distract the audience.

Videos are a less satisfactory way of communicating with an international audience. If a video is essential, prepare the audience for what they will see, and show only a few minutes at a time. Showing a video longer than about ten minutes is tempting fate. International audiences can rapidly get lost in the soundtrack. (Be sure to bring exactly the right type of video for the technology of the country you are visiting.)

Prepare some back-up aids in case technology lets you down. Posters are fine. Flip charts are fine. A whiteboard is fine. Write short phrases in large, neat letters.

Strangely, I have seen Westerners give presentations abroad that are spectacularly sloppy. The presenters appear to stumble in and improvise a conversation on the hoof. Perhaps they expect an international audience to be awestruck by their miraculous ability to speak the English language. Of course, the opposite is true. With an international audience, anything less than a thoroughly professional approach will provoke a cool response.

So be scrupulously professional in your presentation – but be human too.

Be yourself

You are more than a representative of your company or your country: you are a person too. So within the formality guidelines (please, no irony! no T-shirts! no sneakers!) trust yourself and be yourself. Remember that in Asia particularly, human relationships are the basis of all successful business deals. This requires us to be human beings – not just robots in presentation mode.

What's your style? Are you exceedingly, even quaintly formal? Fine – carry on that way. Do you favour Mickey Mouse ties with your pinstripe suit? You can get away with that. Are you a terrible amateur artist? Provided they're relevant to your topic, freehand drawings will delight even the most august academic audiences.

In some contexts, you can introduce pictures of your home and family without being self-indulgent or unprofessional. For example, at the 1994 national conference of the Japan Secretaries Association I showed a photograph of myself and my five sisters as children, all dressed alike and lined up in steps and stairs. The emotional engagement of the audience rose steeply as the picture appeared. I used this family photograph legitimately to illustrate career path patterns of New Zealand women over three decades.

Whatever your style, do allow your real self to show through your careful, formal presentation. Your personality is probably your greatest asset.

Use written translations wisely

If we are speaking to an audience of mixed nationalities (for example at an international conference) then providing a written translation of a speech is not much use. But often, the audience shares a language – for example if we are visiting a company in Thailand. Then we can reduce the audience's pain and strain by the judicious use of a written translation.

You might choose to provide translations of:

- your company profile or other PR documents
- the captions on your slides
- the short outline of your speech or presentation.

Beware of the urge to translate every document indiscriminately. If we don't know the other language, we cannot discuss the translated document. (Often the translator has made significant changes, unbeknownst to us.) Global English is better for two-way communication, unless we are truly bilingual.

Learn how to work with interpreters

At business meetings or presentations, you can arrange for an oral interpreter to translate what you are saying on the spot. Wonderful! Wonderful? Only if you work together effectively.

If you follow the principles of Global English in your speech, your interpreter will be delighted. Global English eliminates all the factors in English that are impossible or difficult to translate.

If you use an oral interpreter:

- cut the length of your speech by at least half
- give the interpreter a copy of your speech several days in advance
- agree on how much you will say before the interpreter takes over (about two or three sentences is right)
- look at the audience, not at the interpreter, while the interpreter is speaking.

10

Global English on the World Wide Web

Bear in mind that you may be dealing with people who use English as a second or third language. It can be easy to get your wires crossed.

David Merritt and Paul Reynolds

This chapter focuses on how to make Web pages more attractive to the one billion people who use English as a second (or alternative) language.

With the explosion of interest in the Internet, the words 'language' and 'writing' have taken on new meaning. 'Language' means html or Java or somesuch. 'Writing' means putting carrot marks and slashes in the right places.

In any large bookshop you can now find metres of shelves about how to 'write' Web pages. Inside a very small percentage of these manuals (maybe five per cent?) you will find a few paragraphs about what kind of English to use in a Web page. And I can assert with moderate confidence that you will find not one word about how to write English that is easy for people all over the world to understand.

This is peculiar (to put it very politely), because the Internet is global by definition.

The English text is the downfall of many a Web page. Internet users often turn off the graphics. Then the only thing left is words. If Web surfers have to pause and puzzle over one sentence on our home page, we've lost them forever. If our words are difficult to understand, we have wasted all that expense, expertise, enterprise and effort.

Misunderstandings on the Internet can provoke violent reactions. Global English ensures we say exactly what we mean. Then we're less likely to get flamed for something we didn't mean to say.

We know that Internet users are happy to read text – but not if it's confusing or dull. If you're writing a Web page in English and you want people in Asia and Russia and Eastern Europe to read it, you had better read this chapter. The two essentials are to use Global English, and to provide a suitable structure and signposts.

Internet users are:

- educated
- volatile
- information-hungry
- very, very numerous
- wealthier than average
- not necessarily native English speakers.

At least 40 million people vault impulsively around the Internet seeking interesting material to read. On the World Wide Web they have millions of home pages to visit.

Internet users are not captive readers. We have one chance to capture the attention of these sophisticated, selective readers. Our copy has to be very, very good – or the Internet users immediately jump to another site.

We have to use our neck-top computers to get the language right.

Structuring Web pages

The computer speaks English.

It is no use structuring language on the Internet as if it were language on paper. Unlike the printed media, language on the Internet is:

- non-sequential (pieces can be encountered in any order)
- non-hierarchical (we can apply the 'first things first' rule only to individual chunks, not to the document as a whole)
- modular (text consists of small self-contained interlocking chunks)
- interconnected (text is linked to other sites)
- without beginning or end
- temporary.

Other factors affecting Web structure

- Reading costs money (so readers won't persevere with confusing, boring or irrelevant text).
- Readers are constantly invited by link words to abandon your text.
- Readers can contact the writer.
- Readers can see only one screen at a time.
- Readers can change the fonts (so the structure must be clear regardless of design).

Obviously, then, text for the World Wide Web must be structured differently from words in print. Writing for the Web means writing in chunks with many clear signposts. People from a different language background require an especially strict structure to keep them on track.

On the Web, time and megabytes are money. So the significance of your page must be immediately obvious to browsers. Otherwise they won't continue reading, they won't download, and they won't return to your site.

The following methods will give your Web page an appropriate structure, and make non-English-speaking people feel welcome.

Use a modular structure for Web pages

We cannot assume that people will read our pages from go to whoa. They might read only one short paragraph. So every paragraph must make sense alone.

Don't think of your pages as having a certain sequence. The virtual structure of your text is constantly divaricating – dividing into two again and again and again and again....

Therefore, structure Web writing in modules, or chunks, with frequent explanatory headings. A chunk may be one paragraph, or two or three short paragraphs.

Think in paragraphs

A well-constructed Global English paragraph on a Web page:

- makes sense and is worth reading even out of context
- is a single unit of thought
- has one to five short sentences
- may include a bulleted list

- begins with a topic sentence or an explanatory heading.

TRY THIS

As an experiment, write one paragraph for a Web page about your company, or some other organisation. Check that it follows the guidelines above.

How long is a Web page?

A Web page can be any length at all. If you want your pages to be read by non-English-speaking people, it's usually better to have short pages – just one or two screens per page.

An ideal Web page has a balanced mix of headings, text, graphics and empty space.

When writing text, think not in pages but in screens. How many words can you comfortably read on a 14-inch screen? For most situations, a comfortable amount of text on a Web screen is roughly 50–100 words. This might be two or three short paragraphs.

People from non-English-speaking backgrounds can be repelled by Web pages that are too long. To view a very long page, users have to scroll... and scroll... and scroll.... That can be maddening, even for native English speakers.

Web pages that are too cryptic are equally annoying. Even on a contents page, include a few short explanatory phrases.

Choose link words and phrases with care

Clickable link words or phrases are like rockets that transport users to another site. When you choose your link words, always keep your international clients in mind. Choose link words that:

- have only one clear meaning
- are significant to people with various language backgrounds.

Separate link words from text whenever possible

Link words can either be highlighted within the text, or placed separately from the text (as icons or words).

The second option is better for your international clients. For their sake, place the link words in a separate spot from the text whenever possible – at the start or end of the page, or in a margin, or between paragraphs, or near graphics.

The first option, highlighting words within a text, is likely to distract international readers from the act of reading. Highlighted link words within the text are like traffic signals that are all flashing 'Go!' They can dazzle the eyes, wreck the concentration and create an option glut.

Example

In the following excerpt from a Web page, the link words 'visual feedback' are separated from the text.

✔ At a business meeting, you can see whether you are being understood. By contrast, when you write, visual feedback and voice tone are missing.

visual feedback

Clicking the underlined, separated phrase visual feedback will lead to more detail about the information conveyed by facial expression and body language.

TRY THIS

Which word would you use as a link word or phrase after the following paragraph? You can either select the word(s) from the paragraph, or write a new phrase. Suggest what information the link would lead to.

Follow-up visits are very important. Failure to keep follow-up appointments could jeopardise a good result. Routine follow-up appointments are at one day after laser treatment, one week, one month, three months, six months and one year. All of these appointments are included in the surgical fee that is paid in full prior to laser eye surgery.

Provide plenty of explanatory headings

Because you want your Web pages to be truly 'worldwide', be lavish with headings. Headings are a comfort. Headings are helpful. Headings give context. Headings are essential.

Wherever a Web page includes text, there should be at least two explanatory headings on every screen. Users should always be able to see at least two headings, no matter where they are scrolling and no matter how small their window. Write all headings in Global English.

Design a truly worldwide page

Reading English on a screen is oh so exhausting for people who didn't learn English at their mother's knee. So on your Web page, provide lots of empty space to rest their eyes. Always leave a line between paragraphs.

Use the standard font sizes for the Web. Keep design very simple. Your page can still look beautiful, and clarity should be top priority.

TRY THIS

Just for fun, roughly design a heading for a Web page. Make the heading (or banner) absolutely clear and simple and easy to read.

11

Global English for business with Asia

Business executives throughout the world suffer from International Communications Disorder, but there is no trading area on earth in which the ailment is more prevalent than in the Asia-Pacific region.

David L. James

This chapter concentrates specifically on the use of English for communication with Asian people.

The dramatic rise of the economies of Asia means that nowadays millions of English-speaking people want to trade with Asia, visit Asia or enter into dialogue with Asian people. And Asia has come to meet the West, in the form of Asian tourists, professional people, investors and businesspeople travelling the globe.

'Asia' is a convenient way of referring to an enormous area of the planet Earth. Asia is not one homogeneous culture, but includes many countries of astonishing diversity. In this chapter, 'Asia' refers to South East and North Asia. (The advice is not so relevant to South Asia, the Indian sub-continent.)

- South East Asia (Indonesia, Thailand, Cambodia, Myanmar, Laos, the Philippines, Vietnam, Singapore and Malaysia).
- North Asia (China, Japan, Hong Kong, Korea and Taiwan).

What to expect when communicating with Asian people

Many Westerners are slightly nervous about dealing with people from South East and North Asia, because the cultures are unfamiliar to them. Generalisations are dangerous, I know, but the following points are worth bearing in mind before you begin communicating with people in Asia.

Your Asian business clients and professional colleagues are likely to be:

- nervous about using English
- courteous
- in no hurry to sign a deal
- reluctant to lose face
- very conscious of hierarchies
- unwilling to do business with a stranger
- primarily interested in their relationship with you.

Decisions in Asia are often made by consensus. Long meetings and discussions precede decision-making. Everything we send in writing to Asia is likely to be studied by many people. So we had better write very clearly and concisely: any misunderstanding is compounded by the number of people involved.

In general, Asian people do not appreciate individualism, self-promotion and pushiness. They value service and quality very highly, even ahead of price. They want to build a long-term relationship with their business partners. If we show impatience, they may feel embarrassed for us because we have lost control. And in some Asian countries, a display of anger is regarded as shameful in the extreme.

All these factors lurk in the background as we pick up the telephone to call somebody Asian, or compose a letter or report to send to Asia.

These generalisations are only a starting point, and no substitute for studying the culture of a particular country. Each country has its own accepted level of formality and its own customs.

And everybody in Asia is an individual, of course. From the very start, you may encounter people who completely contradict the stereotype. Who knows? Your first Asian colleague may be a casual, impatient, eccentric, Westernised, wannabe hippie.

Nevertheless, the generalisations are a useful reference point. When we hit a communication barrier, we may find we have offended against some of the underlying values of an Asian culture.

The following tips will help you to steer safely through the cultural reefs of Asia.

Tips for communicating with Asian people

Boasting is repulsive.
Claude C. Hopkins

When communicating with Asian people:

- use Global English
- summarise oral discussions in writing
- ask for clarification when necessary
- read between the lines for a hidden 'no'.

At all times, be conscious of courtesy:

- apologise if you need to
- pay attention to personal relations: they are top priority
- use surnames always, with Mr, Miss, Mrs, or Dr
- show your status.

Never:

- speak badly of anyone – in your own company, or a competitor's company, or the Asian company
- hint that someone else is at fault
- push hard for a 'yes' or 'no'
- use jokes or assume intimacy.

There's a (very important) time and place for courtesy

Asian languages are often deliberately gentle and vague. Does this mean that you should also be gentle and vague in all your communications? Oh no! Clarity should always be the goal.

Certainly the personal relationship is of primary importance when communicating with people from Asia. But keep it in its place, literally. With letters, use a personal touch in your first and final paragraphs – the courtesy paragraphs. In between, stick to business. When you are in consultation abroad, take your cue from your Asian hosts. Notice how they start with social chitchat, then subtly signal that now it is time for business. Social engagements from karaoke to golf are almost compulsory. Sometimes a business discussion arises over drinks or dinner – but wait for the Asian person to raise the topic of business first, and don't regard that discussion as binding.

Safe topics for personal conversation include family, home, weather, education, holidays and shared experiences. Talk politics?

I'd rather do the polka in a minefield. Asian people may be very critical of their own governments and nevertheless resent our comments as outsiders. Even discussing the politics of our own country can be tricky. We should not even hint that our government is superior. Yet if we criticise our country, Asians may think we are either unpatriotic or truly bizarre.

Separate business from courtesy

Courtesy demands its own paragraphs, its own time slot. We can be clear, even blunt, in business discussions, provided we start and end with paragraphs (or a few minutes' talk) devoted exclusively to personal interest and interaction.

By numbering the business points in a letter, or by using bullets, we can signal the end of personal interaction and the start of business.

Examples of courtesy paragraphs

- ✔ Thank you for your New Year greetings. I am glad to hear that you have returned from your travels safely. We are all very pleased that you found your recent visit to New Zealand useful.
- ✔ I hope your business is prospering.
- ✔ I look forward to continuing our dialogue, and developing the relationship between our two companies. Please convey my best wishes to Mr Shen.

TRY THIS

Write a short, simple, sincere courtesy paragraph. Either have a real Asian client in mind, or just invent a person and a situation.

Be clear and concise

Clarity and courtesy are the essentials when writing for Asia. Think of clarity as an expression of your courtesy.

Many Westerners are so sensitive about the need to be courteous to Asian people that they get into a double-bind. Trying to be polite, they pad their speech and writing with meaningless fluffy phrases. Wordiness makes the message incomprehensible. They've got the right motivation (be polite) but the wrong solution (be incomprehensible).

Letters full of long-winded phrases are much harder for Asian readers to understand.

Example

✖ It would be useful if you could give an indication of the sort of resources you might be able to apply to the project so we can best target any funding available for setting up the training centre and the sort of resources it might need.

Notice that the 'courteous' sentence above has the dreadfully high EFLAW® score of 70. The writer intended to be deeply courteous. As a result, this 'business' sentence is so vague as to be almost meaningless. Indeed, the wish to show respect is one main reason why wordy phrases are used.

Don't use jokes or assume intimacy

It is always safer to be too formal than too informal when doing business with Asia. That means no horsing around. Well, not until you have known a particular person for about 50 years.

Jokes in English are almost inevitably misunderstood by people from other cultures. Jokes can cause confusion and distress. If we tell a joke, we often seem like an idiot, frankly. Irony and sarcasm are almost certain to be taken at face value. This means Asian clients will get exactly the opposite meaning from what we really intended with our little joke. (Remember, too, that many other people may read that casual letter you write to a close business associate.)

Use the right technology and stationery

For your first personal contact with an Asian organisation, a short formal letter is usually the best way to communicate. High quality white paper with a well-designed letterhead makes an excellent impression in Asia. Show your phone and fax numbers in the international way, with a plus sign before the country code.

The preferred style of communication in Asia is the face-to-face meeting.

Be wary of urging an Asian company or individual to respond by fax or phone until you know their preferences. As the relationship develops, you may find that your Asian contact prefers to communicate by fax. In this case, reply by fax. If the Asian person uses snail mail, reply by snail mail. Budgets, technology and other factors are all significant in the choice.

Your Asian client may habitually use a different size of paper from your company. For this reason, check that your fax has nothing important at the bottom of the page: that part can be lost when your document is photocopied.

International toll calls can be awkward for both parties, with problems of expense, time zones, language and connections. Arranging the call in advance can reduce the difficulties.

Check and double-check that you are using the correct names, addresses and titles of your Asian correspondents. When you receive a letter, don't throw away the envelope: this may be the only place where the sender writes the return address.

TRY THIS

Write your own name and address and phone number in a way that is acceptable and comprehensible in Asia.

Writing letters to Asia

When you are writing letters to Asia, remember these points:

- write in formal, Global English
- start and end with a courtesy paragraph
- separate the courtesy paragraphs from the central, clear message
- show patience
- refer to your correspondent's colleagues and yours, where appropriate
- state the date as day: month (spelled out in full): year.

(See the guidelines for the structure of faxes and letters on page 71.)

Example: an inappropropriate letter to Asia

✖ 12.1.1996

Dear Mr Tanaka

I have received your order for 2,000 Alucatch window fastenings, Type 5XXA. You didn't say what colour you wanted. Please fax details immediately. Thank you.

Yours sincerely

John Brown

An appropriate letter to Asia

✔ 1 December 1996

Dear Mr Tanaka

YOUR ORDER – ALUCATCH WINDOW FASTENINGS

Thank you for your kind messages and the news from Yokohama. I was delighted to hear about your daughter Masumi's success in job-hunting.

1. We were delighted to receive your order for 2 000 Alucatch window fastenings, Type 5XXA.
2. We can despatch this order on 7 December by DHL courier.
3. Would you please advise us by fax what colours you require? Colours available are Black, White, Silver and Bronze.

We are sorry to bother you with extra work, knowing you are very busy.

Please give my regards to Mr Yukio and Mr Murayama.

Yours sincerely

John Brown
Manager, Despatch Section

Notice the following improvements in the second letter:

- the main point is in the subject line
- the letter starts and ends with a courtesy paragraph
- the points are numbered
- the date is in the correct format.

Notice also:

- the removal of any hint of blame
- the apology for causing trouble
- the positive tone
- the mention of colleagues
- the signature showing the writer's status in the company.

12

Changing your company's international communication style

Team learning is vital because teams, not individuals, are the fundamental learning unit in modern organisations. This is where 'the rubber meets the road'; unless teams can learn, the organisation cannot learn.
Peter Senge

The future demands that we use Global English in many situations. The chances are that our success depends on it.

It's true – today the world is a global village. No matter what our business, most of us are in contact with people from other countries. People are vigorously communicating across barriers of nationality, geography and language.

If you work in a company or organisation that deals with people from a non-English-speaking background, it's not enough for you alone to know about Global English. Your colleagues also need some training. The stakes are high. Your company should be using Global English for:

- every fax, letter, proposal or report that is sent overseas
- all international business communication, written or oral
- dialogue with tourists and immigrants
- advertisements in international publications
- instructions and user-manuals for exported goods
- international speeches and presentations.

What's the next step? You've virtually finished reading this book. You understand the basic principles of Global English. You have learned how to write effective letters to international clients and how to give successful speeches in an international setting. In fact, you've learned the secret code. Now you're ready to apply this new knowledge to every international document and meeting.

The next step is to spread the secret code of Global English throughout your company or organisation. A strategic programme of editing and training is required.

Without a company-wide programme of support, writing Global English can be a lonely and frustrating task. At this moment, you may be the only person around who knows the code. You'll see letters and reports and pamphlets leaving your company that will be misunderstood by international clients. You can see that poor communication is costing your company money.

Ultimately, it is necessary to adjust the international communication style of the whole company. The goal is to ensure that every international communication produced by the company is crystal clear to the receiver. A small company can achieve a great deal by providing Global English training for every staff member who has contact with international clients.

In a large company, many people will be involved in planning the change – the international marketing manager, communications manager and human resources manager, for example. The company might go through the following stages:

- incorporate Global English principles into the company's quality assurance programme
- train the communications manager and editors in Global English
- have Global English editors rewrite all standard letters and documents that go to international clients
- provide in-house training for key personnel
- provide a check-list and style guide for all personnel
- train key personnel in other towns by e-mail.

The rewards of a Global English training programme arrive rapidly. As soon as the programme is launched, staff become sensitised to the needs of international readers. That's the big breakthrough.

Before training, the attitude of staff is often one of exasperation with clients from non-English-speaking backgrounds. 'Why can't they understand? Why can't they use English properly?' Sometimes there is even a touch of condescension. 'Are they stupid or what?' After training, staff understand there is much they can do to ease communication. This realisation can come as a considerable relief.

Consolidating your Global English skills

I hear and I forget. I see and I remember. I do and I understand.
Old Chinese saying

Within large companies and organisations, maintaining the time-saving, money-saving culture of Global English is a managerial responsibility. Ideally, the team gets and gives full support through a company-wide programme.

People who work alone or who don't have the support of a quality assurance programme may feel they need some help in learning and consolidating Global English skills. The good news is that if you remember even two Global English principles, this will still affect your international communication very positively.

The principles of Global English are easy to apply after a certain period of practice. Eventually the habits become deeply ingrained, second nature. This is the goal.

To get there, we have to practise – fine. To practise, we have to remember to practise. In the real world, we need a methodical approach and support from a buddy until we can write Global English automatically.

Use memory joggers

A simple trick is to write some of the principles of Global English on cards. Put one or two cards where you'll see them daily – for example, on your computer desk, in your wallet , in your diary or by the phone.

Change the cards every few days. (Otherwise you'll stop seeing them.)

Examples of memory joggers

Lower the EFLAW® score.

Write short sentences.

Use words with one clear meaning.

Put the main point first.

Avoid hidden metaphors.

Use formal one-word verbs.

Use positive language.

Write explanatory headings.

Repeat key words.

Enunciate all consonants.

Number your paragraphs.

TRY THIS

Write a few more memory joggers that would be useful to you. Which of the memory joggers would you use first?

Find a buddy-editor

Find a buddy-editor who is also using Global English. Check each other's international documents. Practise your speeches on each other. Make it a regular, automatic habit. What you miss, your buddy will notice – and vice versa.

Train by e-mail

You can enrol for a personal training programme in Global English. For convenience, you study at your own place and your own pace, and are tutored by e-mail.

An important part of the training course is free, confidential editorial advice on some of your company's documents.

Use Global English software

'EFLAW® : The Global English Editor' is new software that helps you to edit your international documents into Global English.

For information about training or software, e-mail mcalpr@netlink.co.nz

Global English checklist

Word choice

- ☐ Use words with one clear meaning.
- ☐ Use one-word verbs, not phrasal verbs.
- ☐ Use a minimum of miniwords.
- ☐ Repeat key words and phrases.
- ☐ Avoid hidden metaphors and idiomatic expressions.
- ☐ Use positive language.
- ☐ Use plenty of action verbs.

Sentence construction

- ☐ Use short sentences (maximum: 20 words).
- ☐ Put only one idea in a sentence.
- ☐ Use full stops liberally in written text.
- ☐ Use the classic English sentence order: somebody-does-something.
- ☐ Start every sentence with the main subject.

Questions

- ☐ Ask questions that are very simple.
- ☐ Phrase questions in a positive way.

Structure, format and layout

- ☐ Structure predictably and clearly.
- ☐ Put a summary (or the main point) first or second.
- ☐ Start and end every letter with a courtesy paragraph.
- ☐ Start every paragraph with a topic sentence.
- ☐ Number the paragraphs (or in letters, key points).
- ☐ Use plenty of explanatory headings.
- ☐ Use conventional fonts and plenty of white space.

Style Sheet

- ☐ Note words that international clients use differently from you.
- ☐ Note the key words that you choose, and stick to them.

The final touches to an international document

Prooofread with your international readers in mind

Whoopsie! 'Prooofread'? Many of our international clients are more skilled in spelling, grammar and punctuation than the average native English speaker. They may notice little errors, and judge us harshly. Proofread extra carefully.

Shortcut to perfect punctuation: use full stops

In Global English, the most useful and foolproof punctuation mark is the full stop (otherwise known as the period). Use full stops liberally in your writing, and give them every encouragement to multiply – the more the merrier. If you find yourself wondering whether to insert a comma or a full stop, quit worrying. The answer is always the same: use a full stop. They help you to keep your sentences short. And they will short-circuit many a grammar mistake.

What is the purpose in life of the humble comma? It is to eliminate ambiguity or confusion.

Examples

✔ In the sea below, the rocks looked very small.

✔ According to Mother, Father will be late.

In Global English, it's better to use a pair of brackets than a pair of commas. The words between two commas are regarded as a 'nice to know' item which readers can safely skip. This convention can be confusing for international readers, because it interrupts the flow of thought.

Examples

✖ The stairs, they noted, were of industrial steel.

✔ They noted that the stairs were of industrial steel.

✖ Kidnapped Hong Kong film director Au Fook-hung, known to movie fans as Chung Shiu-hung, left Guangzhou under the escort of several public security guards.

✔ Kidnapped Hong Kong film director Au Fook-hung left Guangzhou escorted by several public security guards. (Au Fook-hung is known to movie fans as Chung Shiu-hung.)

The comma splice is probably the commonest punctuation error made by native English speakers. Comma splices join two sentences with a comma. Without getting too picky, just remember that when in doubt, use a full stop (not a comma).

Example

✖ Most people use 14-inch monitors, they don't use 23-inch monitors.

✔ Most people use 14-inch monitors. They don't use 23-inch monitors.

Use a clear and simple format

The right format or design is hugely helpful for your international clients. Keep design very simple, conventional and uncluttered: that's the main rule.

Conventional layout and fonts are best for Global English. Any unusual design may interfere with comprehension. Simple Roman characters may already seem rather exotic to people who grew up with Chinese characters. Curb the creative impulse. Don't complicate matters with fancy fonts and jiggly designs.

Provide plenty of white space: non-English-speaking readers need quiet places to rest their anxious eyes. About 12 words per line is plenty. Leave a blank line between paragraphs, and use bullet points when appropriate.

Global English text should not be *spattered* with *individual* words or phrases in italics. *Italics* make the *surrounding* text hard to read. In *general*, it is *better* to *emphasise* a point by using bold or a larger font size.

A LARGE BLOCK OF CAPITAL LETTERS IS SURPRISINGLY HARD TO READ. ALL THE LETTERS ARE THE SAME SIZE SO THE READER LACKS THE CLUES OF VARYING SIZE.

TRY THIS

Here's one more exercise to try. What's wrong with this passage as a piece of Global English? How would you rewrite it to make it easy for international readers?

The Council comprises 35 members representing exporters of primary commodities and manufactured exports to Korea, importers of a range of products from Korea, and a number of service related companies.

Further reading

A vigorous discussion about English can be found in Bill Bryson's *Mother Tongue* (1990, Avon Books, New York).

An excellent guide to doing business in Asia is David L. James' book, *The Executive Guide to Asia-Pacific Communications* (Allen & Unwin, Sydney, 1995).

The Global Speaker: an English Speaker's Guide to Making Presentations Around the World by Patricia L. Kurtz (amacom, New York, 1995) gives detailed advice about giving speeches in an international context. The main focus is Europe, not Asia.

Anyone interested in communicating with a particular culture will benefit from studying (even briefly) a simple grammar book of the language concerned. This will reveal many specific instances of possible misunderstandings. A bilingual dictionary is another great asset: the best words to use are the words in that dictionary.

Studying a standard book that teaches EFL (English as a foreign language) to business people will reinforce the principles of Global English.

Linguists and teachers of English are involved in a red-hot, ongoing debate about the ever-changing roles of English in the world. Internet users can catch up with the 'world Englishes' debate by seeking first the sites of ATESOL, TESOL, TESL-EJ and JALT.

On page 8 of this book, the source of the figures about the costs of poor communication are:

- Australian and Canadian figures from 'Poor reading, writing skills costing millions' by Mark Henderson, *Sunday Star Times*, 1 September 1996.
- British figures from 'Discover your wordpower' by Graham King, *The Sunday Times*, 24 April 1994.
- EC figures from Bill Bryson's *Mother Tongue*.
  (Costs are quoted in New Zealand dollars.)

On page 11, estimates are given for the number of people who speak English in the world. These can only be estimates, of course. In an e-mail message to Jane Hoelker (JALT National Program Chair) the distinguished linguist Braj Kachru says that estimates vary from

800 million (of whom about 57% are non-native users) to two billion users. He adds that 'There is also another rather rough estimate according to which there are three to four non-native users for every native user.'

Information about the numbers in China's elementary school pilot programme was gathered from a lecture at JALT 1994 by Professor Liu Daoyi (Vice President of Curriculum & Teaching Materials Research Institute, and President of National Foreign Language Teaching Association, Education Society of China).

Answers to 'Try this' exercises

Note that every exercise has many possible answers. Compare your answers with these.

Page 7

The sentence is too long and complex. 'Kick off' is a metaphor whose meaning is not obvious.

Obludu District Council planners have apparently bungled. Their bungle has been identified as one of the key reasons why the Dianeville City Centre project could not start in March. The late start means the project is too late to take advantage of positive market forces. Consequently, the Obludu New Enterprise Trust is now in financial difficulties.

Page 15

The EFLAW® score of the passage is 50: far too high for non-English-speaking readers to understand easily. By rewriting the sentence as two, we reduce the EFLAW® score to 18.5.

I enjoy the notion of well-paid, well-informed consultants working for me (though I am slightly sceptical about their abilities). Therefore I invested modestly in the sharemarket recently.

Page 18

The conference facilities are available on 23–24 July.

'Free' has several possible meanings. A non-English-speaking person might think that there would be no charge for the use of conference facilities on those dates.

Page 20

You must return this form.

Page 21

'This is the last one she has got' could mean anything! Perhaps:

The enclosed diary is the last available 'Wild Flowers' diary.

Page 22

People are becoming slightly bored.

Page 24

The council is often at fault. However, this time the council may be correct.

Page 26

The sentences with action verbs are:

2 The Council zoned the area industrial.

3 They are suffering from malnutrition.

Page 27

Significantly fewer crimes were reported in Crumpville. This reduction contradicts the national trend.

Page 28

1 let out: release

2 give up: surrender

3 come along with: accompany

4 give away: reveal.

Page 30

I will **check** the programme, **study** the timetable and **make** the reservations.

Page 32

1 We intend to do this, *or* we plan to do this, *or* we promise to do this.

2 I'm sorry, I do not have the authority to do this.

Page 33

Albatross Aviation has been operating continuously for over 20 years. CEO Susan Dufresne says that Albatross Aviation is about to acquire three more twin-engined planes.

Page 35

1 physically around the corner

2 the same distance away as the horizon

3 before the tax officer cuts and kicks a person

4 something to do with rays of light or soundwaves

5 putting a harness on.

Page 40

1 Our client has been treated with impeccable fairness.

2 Our policy is to help endangered languages to recover and to grow stronger.

3 You shouldn't try to sell goods on your first trip abroad.
4 There is a high demand for finished leather.
5 'Great creative talent is essential for success in advertising,' commented an experienced advertising man.

Page 43

The Whitetown Community Interpreting Service Incorporated provides interpreting services. This ensures that members of the community who are not native speakers of English can understand information. Interpreters also help people to express themselves clearly, so that they are understood.

Non-English-speaking consumers can use your service only if they can communicate fully with your staff. They can be wrongly diagnosed. They can sign forms they do not understand. They can misunderstand instructions for further appointments or treatment. They can misunderstand instructions for their child's school or health needs.

Page 47

Payment in advance or open account trading is common in Australia. This system has certain problems. If you pay in advance, you may not see the goods before you pay. Also, you will not receive title to the goods until the transport documents arrive.

Page 50

According to *The Net* magazine (July 1995) the average users of the World Wide Web are:

- 25 to 55 years old
- high earners (average income of NZ$120 000 per annum)
- highly educated (95% have at least four years tertiary education).

Page 51

1 improvement of mountain bike trails
2 seminar for check-out supervisors
3 customers of power companies.

Page 54

The SEZs must maintain their distinctiveness, said Western business executives in Beijing. To do so, the SEZs must offer something that other parts of the country cannot.

Page 55

1 Roget first proposed his system of verbal classification 190 years ago.
2 One pair of rats can produce 100 000 descendants within three years. Scientists have proved this conclusively.

Page 56

Higher imports overshadowed the earnings of foreign currencies. Imports were higher because import duties were reduced and because exports grew more slowly.

Page 58

In some disciplines there seems to be nothing more to discover. Perhaps the clearest example is geographical exploration—a possible exception being the deep ocean trenches.

Page 60

Mr Ondaatje said he would also ask the National People's Congress to investigate. (Mr Ondaatje is a delegate to the Congress.)

Page 63

Mr Lowe counted the competing commercial radio stations and reached the extraordinary tally of 156. He noted that other types of media were also competing with radio companies.

Page 65

1 Does your company need insurance? If so, please contact agent Ray Tommison at +64 6 387 4312.

2 At 31 January 1996, 1400 professional firemen were employed nationally. Do you think that number should be

☐ increased ☐ maintained ☐ decreased? (tick one)

Page 66

1 The person who says 'Yes' is agreeing that the infrastructure of Kobe is not yet fully restored.

Page 66

Taiwanese teachers showed a strong interest in the Bannerbook and Kidbook series. They considered that the Kidbook series in particular was culturally suitable for their students.

Page 68

Individual answers.

Page 72

A problem of this magnitude probably demands a personal visit. The original abrupt letter might well destroy an international business relationship. The person should be addressed by name, of course.

Dear Mr Kim

I hope you and Mrs Kim are well, and that your business is prospering despite the recent typhoon.

I am very sorry to tell you that yesterday we found some minor contamination in one batch of MooCow vanilla ice-cream. A few sesame seeds had apparently fallen into the rich dairy cream that is the basis of MooCow icecream.

Please check your shelves. If you have any products from Batch #NP856, please destroy them as a precaution. Please keep a record of the number of containers you had to destroy, if any.

Next week I will fly to Seoul to discuss the problem with you personally.

We will refund your money or replace the products immediately, whichever you prefer.

We have investigated the problem, and have now implemented extra quality control procedures to prevent a reoccurrence.

Please accept our sincere apologies for this great inconvenience. We value your custom very highly, as you know. As a token of our goodwill, today we are despatching a sample of our new product.

Kind regards

Michael Angelo

Managing Director

Page 73

Instead of the first sentence (I needed to take control of my life), start with:

When I gave up smoking, I regained control of my life and my finances.

Page 75

The best speakers are true to themselves

(or) Be yourself

Page 75

We have compared the advantages of e-mail with the advantages of the fax. The disadvantages of faxes are:

- cost
- thermal paper
- paper size.

Pages 78, 83 and 90

Individual exercises

Page 91

Depending on the structure of your pages, a good link phrase might be surgical fee.

Page 92 and 96

Individual exercises

Page 98

Have you written your name and address in a way that is acceptable and comprehensible in Asia? It's best to:

- include your title (President, Administration Manager, etc.)
- omit commas and full stops
- include postal code
- write a plus sign before the phone number
- follow the plus sign with the international code.

In some cases you might include your academic qualifications.

Page 103

Extra memory joggers might include:

- Structure speeches rigidly
- Speak slowly
- Take care with pronouns
- Start and end with courtesy paragraphs

– or many other items. Express them however you wish.

Whichever memory jogger you choose to use first is the best one for you to start with.

Page 106

The sentence is too long. Using bullets would make it easier to understand.

The Council has 35 members. They represent:

- exporters of primary commodities to Korea
- exporters of manufactured goods to Korea
- importers of products from Korea
- service-related companies.

Advanced exercises

Chapter 1

Find the EFLAW® score of the following sentences.
Rewrite sentences 3 and 4 to lower their EFLAW® scores.

1 Thank you for your New Year greetings.

2 I am very pleased you found your recent visit to Washington useful.

3 We will also prepare some preliminary ideas on the education centre based on our past experience in developing similar centres in the South Pacific and Asia.

4 I would just like to take this opportunity to confirm and clarify our understanding of the proposal and the role of each of our organisations in progressing the proposal.

Chapter 2

Rewrite the following sentences in Global English. Reduce the proportion of miniwords, remove all unnecessary words, and remove all words that might cause difficulty for international readers. (You may need to invent information or guess at the meaning.)

5 In view of the fact that the consensus of opinion holds the Minister responsible, the victim's accusation could not be more untrue.

6 When it's over, they'll ask him to let them publish it.

7 It is noted that they are not written in Global English, so they compound the problem.

8 If he hasn't got it, phone them right away.

9 Inasmuch as this figure is slightly less than 10% of average yearly housing starts, annual nationwide housing starts might expand roughly 3% more than they otherwise would.

10 Bay of Islands man on to it. Professional, 45 yrs old who loves the Lord seeks tall on to it feminine attractive lady.

11 In looking outward to the movements in standards of living among neighbours and trading partners, New Zealanders show a keen awareness of the fact that the rises in standards are mainly to be found among the Asian countries, and that historical partners like the United Kingdom and the United States are, or are seen to be, experiencing progressively falling living standards.

12 As I have often gone on record as being critical of the lack of an apparent central strategy for New Zealand Government information, it is a real pleasure being able to redress the balance of the critique by spending some time in the truly excellent new site from Tradenz, the government agency charged with assisting local businesses to take advantage of new export opportunities.

Chapter 3

Find one-word verbs to replace the phrasal verbs below.

13 Phrasal verbs

put up with	use up
take in	drop in
make up	watch out for
give in	get on
come about	take up with

In the following sentences, phrasal verbs are printed in bold. Rewrite the sentences in Global English, replacing phrasal verbs with one-word verbs.

14 The company will **stick to** the original schedule and **make up** the shortfall.

15 Recently we **looked at** the possibility of **getting out of** the contract.

16 When the council set out to improve relations with its sister city, it **set up** the Wellington-Sakai Society.

17 The documentary **went into** the issue of why the Hinds chapter of the Philosophers' Club would not **go along with** the majority decision, and why it subsequently **broke up**.

Rewrite the following sentences making your mood clear.

18 Would you kindly send Form 29D to Mr Kim?

19 The report should be ready on 29 June as scheduled.

20 The last truck-load of milk biscuits could be delayed by the monsoon.

Rewrite the following sentence in Global English. Use short sentences and action verbs.

21 The Government clearly is convinced, and the promised tax cuts are a sign that those who are on the Treasury benches are convinced that economic recovery is well advanced.

Rewrite the following passage in Global English. It has only three complete verbs (in bold). Use more verbs and fewer abstract nouns. Use short sentences.

22 Another factor which **was** an influence in our Executive's decision to publish directories **was** the changed social environment. Restructuring and privatisation of Government departments and agencies, with consequent changes in names and devolution of functions to private and voluntary organisations, Regional Health Authorities, etc., **are** confusing to those in the workforce.

Rewrite the next two sentences in Global English. Use short sentences with more verbs and fewer abstract nouns.

23 My contention is that in so far and for so long as we have such violent phenomena as some one billion people of this world in a starvation position, over 40 000 children dying daily on a global basis, and mass unemployment, racism, poor health and poor educational standards for many, there will always be people and organisations who will organise for radical social change, including Marxists and Marxist parties.

24 In our initial circular letter to Monbusho scholarship alumni, we mentioned that incorporation was really a prerequisite to any corporate sponsorship as well as some support from Gaimusho.

Chapter 4

25 *Rewrite the Web page 'Feeding Our Community the Dream of a Future' on page 39. Use literal language. Eliminate hidden metaphors.*

Chapter 5

Rewrite the following sentences in Global English, breaking up the strings of nouns.

26 Government art work loans will continue.

27 The reactor shipment delay rumours are causing anxiety.

28 The consultants will develop a locality definition framework.

29 Forensic scientists will try to match the new samples with DNA databank rape evidence.

Rewrite the following sentences in Global English. Use the axe: chop each sentence into two or three.

30 Exceptions could be the Philippines and India, which have grown at a relatively sluggish pace and could have faster growth in 1996, but even they could be constrained by inflation and large external deficits.

31 Do you need to get your business licence and make your application to the customs office, with the list of equipment you want to get exemptions on, or can you just have approval and not have applied for the business licence?

32 Both Mr Bax, and chief executive officer of Baring International Bank in London, Peter Norris, have been severely criticised in official reports on the collapse, Mr Bax because he was the man on the spot, and Mr Norris for allegedly contributing to the cover-up and lack of action despite the huge demands for cash being made by Leeson in Singapore as his losses ballooned.

Rewrite the following, correcting the faulty bullet point.

33 In the text of the report Japan appeared as:

- with Korea, the country most frequently perceived to have a rising standard of living (21%)
- after Australia, the best customer for New Zealand's products (67%)
- the foreign language most attractive for New Zealanders to learn (58%).

Rewrite the following paragraph in Global English, using bullet points where appropriate. (This is an advertisement from a hospital.)

34 An Associate Clinical Scientist is required to join the Stem Cell Section of our busy and expanding Department of Histocompatibility and Immunogenetics which at present supports the clinical activities for peripheral blood stem cell harvesting and bone marrow transplantation for hospitals within our region and also supports the London Cord Blood Bank (LCBB).

Rewrite the following paragraph in Global English. Lower the EFLAW® score. Use bullet points to break up the third sentence.

35 More specifically with the Asian community there may be other factors which cause the community in general not to report to the police. Some of the factors which may be identified are such things as: a lack of confidence in the police, which stems from their own socialisation in their originating countries. This lack of confidence may be attributable to all or several of the following factors: poor status of the police in their home country, the police being part of an overt Government agency, police agencies seen as being inferior to other armed forces such as being below the army or the air force, poor training of many police officers in overseas police agencies, corruption both at street level police officers, and on occasion, even at the highest level of police management.

Chapter 6

Rewrite the following sentences in Global English. Use short sentences – 20 words maximum. Put the main point first in each sentence. Repeat key words.

36 Higher imports caused by reduced import duties and slower growth of exports overshadowed the earnings of foreign currencies.

37 Zhuhai has been feeling the pinch from the expected scrapping of preferential policies that have lured domestic and foreign capital and expertise.

38 C & W's new acting chief executive, New Zealander Rod Olson, acknowledged that with three more operators competing for fixed-line service provision in the territory, competition would become harder.

39 While economic reforms have prompted smaller enterprises to think of survival, bigger enterprises are still motivated by policy considerations when it comes to mergers and acquisitions.

40 Through various ingenious devices, sub-contractors and other intermediaries who brought the workers here are found to have siphoned substantial portions of the workers' wages into their own secret accounts.

41 There is a big difference between getting a connection from an Access Provider and actually getting on-line because their system is permanently congested.

42 There are many instances of people being very good at their profession but their business subsequently fails because they did not know how to prepare a full and realistic evaluation of the potential for their proposed business.

Rewrite the following sentences in Global English. Eliminate 'which' and 'that'. Use short sentences.

43 Plentiful food is triggering the early onset of puberty, which causes Hong Kong pre-teens to shoot up in height.

44 The survey, covering youngsters in forms three to five, found their pocket money amounts to more than twice the monthly salary of a Beijing university professor, which is typically around 400 yuan (HK$372) a month.

45 The Planetarium, which was founded in 1968, is a progressive institution which is at the forefront of technical innovation and presentation of modern astronomy as well as being the focus for wide-ranging educational activities.

Rewrite the following sentences in Global English. Use correct punctuation and make any other changes necessary to increase clarity.

46 Japan it is often stated is a land of consensus and there is little doubt these days what the consensus is about: internationalisation.

47 A copy of the proposed application the certificate and a notice of application is sent to all members.

48 From 1 July 1994 all new companies except co-operative companies which apply for incorporation must be registered under the Companies Act 1993.

49 We see present policies as positive, when our clients retire many of them will be on a fixed income so the corrosive effects of inflation must be kept under control.

50 Asynchronous analogue access uses industry standard V.34 modems running on an analogue data circuit in conjunction with a low-cost router to provide a very low cost yet fully functional access to the Internet.

Chapter 7

Rewrite the following sentences in Global English. Eliminate negative expressions wherever possible. Use short sentences.

51 Not only do at least a third of all sitting MPs not know whether they will be back after the next election, but they don't know which party they might not be back for.

52 Your initial market strategy will not be a final statement of objectives, market situations and trends can change rapidly.

53 It will probably not be possible to measure whether cancer control programmes are effective or not until after two decades.

54 People fear that asset testing regimes will not be limited, that estates will be no longer duty-free, that the promise of no capital gains tax will be broken, and that new government schemes will not allow them to safeguard their assets or income.

Chapter 8

Write a topic sentence for each of the following paragraphs. The topic sentence must come first and summarise the main point of the paragraph.

55 The Tata Beach, Golden Bay grower wants throwaway bras to hold his tomatoes and stop their weight breaking trusses from the vines. And this year bras brimming with bright red tomatoes proved a novel Christmas gift. So far Persson has sold more than a dozen fruit-filled bras and now needs replacements. He prefers white and black bras because he reckons they help colour the tomatoes.

56 We can gauge how extensively mediaeval scribes used contractions by comparing MS24 with a modern edition of the same matter: the printed Vulgate occupies some 1340 pages, while the manuscript contains the same text in 876 pages of approximately the same size. Similarly, Boethius On Music fills 200 pages in Freidlein's edition, but only 82 in MS16.

Rewrite the following paragraph in Global English, using short sentences. Write a topic sentence for the paragraph and place it first. Start each sentence with the real subject of the sentence. Repeat key words.

57 The 90-95% reporting rate of all vehicles that are stolen must be contrasted with something like domestic violence, which is a topical issue at the moment and a matter which no doubt many of your readers would have read and seen police publicity about in recent times. Domestic violence may have a true reporting rate of only 8-10% of all crimes.

Rewrite the paragraph below. Use the same word for the same thing. Use bullet points if you like.

58 Because the polio vaccination rate for rural children is far below the 88% national average, a six-year project boosting immunisation of children in

China's poorest areas has been announced. The World Bank will lend China US$100 million to expand immunisation in 10 provinces. The provincial and city governments involved will donate sums equivalent to one-half or one-third of the total investment in the project, which is focusing on the cities of Beijing and Tianjin.

Write explanatory headings for the following paragraphs.

59 The second area of advertising expertise is copywriting. First of all, somebody has to come up with a winning heading. The copy should be clear, easy to follow, crisp and believable. Many people believe that because they can write, they can write copy. There is a huge difference between writing in the English language and writing advertising copy designed to create a desire to buy.

60 The major accidents likely to happen while window cleaning are electrocuting yourself and falling off a ladder. If you touch a powerline with a pole or ladder I don't fancy your chances of making it to your next birthday party other than as char-grilled pork on the buffet table. Please see poles and ladders as potential death traps as soon as you pick them up. A good rule of thumb is always to carry poles and ladders on their side instead of upright, thereby lessening the chance that they will bump into a powerline.

Chapter 9

61 *Think about a proposal, speech or document you might write in the future. Create a structure of one main point with three supporting points. Outline the structure exactly as below, writing one phrase on each line.*

MAIN POINT (summary)

supporting point 1

detail 1.1

detail 1.2

supporting point 2

detail 2.1

detail 2.2

supporting point 3

detail 3.1

detail 3.2

Summary

Chapter 10

62 *Write 100-200 words for a Web page. Decide first what your purpose is – to publicise your company? to sell a product? to generate inquiries? to entertain? or what?*

Select one link word or phrase in each of the following paragraphs. In a few words, suggest what information the link would lead to.

63 I believe it is best to clean the insides of your windows before the outsides for two reasons. Firstly, you want your water to be as clean as possible inside in case you spill some. It will be very dirty by the time you have done all the outsides. The second reason is that most of the spots you'll find on the inside surfaces can be removed without using your scraper. It's great if you can confidently unholster your scraper when you see a spot on the outside – without risking the frustration of discovering the spot is actually on the inside.

64 Eventually you should be able to squeegee an entire window without ever lifting your squeegee off the glass, without leaving a single streak, and without using a rag. This is possibly the most critical section of my instructions, so pay careful attention. Follow these steps and learn the amazing S-stroke which is the key to really fast window cleaning.

65 When your squeegee glides across the glass it acts like a grader pushing gravel around. It scrapes the water off the surface of the glass as it goes along. This water has two choices as to where it goes: it will follow the stronger of two commands. One is the effect of gravity. The other is the grader effect: that is when the water all flows to the end of the squeegee that is being left further behind as you drag it around the glass.

66 Have you ever slaved for hours, rubbing, grinding and polishing your windows only to have your efforts cruelly exposed as inept bumblings the minute the sun shines on them? Do you have an uncanny ability for rearranging an inconspicuous film of dirt into annoying murky streaks? Have you considered hiring a private detective to discover what secret ingredient is used by professional window cleaners to produce a streak-free finish? Then you've come to the right place. We can save you hours of labour and kilojoules of frustration.

Chapter 11

Rewrite the following letters so that they are more appropriate for an Asian business contact. Keep the letters short, clear and courteous. Invent details if necessary.

67 Dear Mr Ng

I will be available for appointments in Singapore on 5-7 September. Can you please arrange a meeting to discuss details of the student exchange scheme between our two schools? Thank you.

Yours sincerely

Roberta Layson

68 Dear Mr Tien

It is now six weeks since I sent a proposal to your company's In-house Publications Manager. As I said at the time, I need a prompt decision on this matter, so that I can pre-order the special paper required. If I don't hear from you by the end of this week, I won't be able to meet your deadline.

Yours sincerely

Don Dovene

69 Dear Yukio

I had a great time in Tokyo with you and the other guys – just don't tell my boss what we got up to! My report is enclosed. I think we made some progress, don't you?

All the best and keep away from those blowfish!

Charles Gross (Charlie to you)

Review Exercise A

The examples of English below would be very difficult for foreign readers to understand. Write comments about each example. What faults can you find? What needs changing?

70 A $53 million loan from the Asia Development Bank to the People's Republic of China for the Hainan Agriculture and Natural Resources Development Project will promote economic growth, reduce rural poverty and the biodiversity and scenic resources of the Jianfengling National Forest Park will be protected.

71 There have been several recent security incidents on World Wide Web servers caused by a rather arcane bug in the workstation portion of the World Wide Web language used to access Web facilities. By not enforcing the length of a Web address, it permitted a knowledgeable user to construct illegitimate service requests by adding additional information.

A fix exists but the problem is symptomatic of the issues which continue to arise in the complexities of the Internet and its services.

72 Bluntly, even with an election possibly just a few months away, the major political parties are dysfunctional. Many MPs, and grassroots party members, are still in the closet, wondering if and when it is safe to come out. This means a number of electoral niches are left unoccupied. There is still an embarrassing silence where radical freemarket policies should be, a hugely pregnant pause where the centrist party should be, a blank page where there should be a Green group, and an empty nest where a Christian party should be.

73 A number of substantial employers retain us on either a retainer or case by case basis to assist with the processing of technical and senior management appointments from overseas. In several circumstances major companies with in-house personnel departments also make use of our services in Immigration related matters. We have associations with management staff selection consultancies, both in Indonesia and overseas.

74 While property loss figures may tend to make the recent earthquake appear to be a relatively minor event economically speaking, other data suggest that its impact in the medium term might be significant. Some government planners tentatively envisage 100 000 new housing units being required over three years. Inasmuch as this figure is slightly less than 10% of average yearly housing starts, annual nationwide housing starts might expand roughly 3% more than they otherwise would. Taking this possibility and others into consideration, the Japan Centre for Economic Research released calculations 27 February that earthquake-related rebuilding would give real gross domestic product a 0.6 percentage point boost in FY 1995, which begins 1 April, and another 0.4 point lift in FY 1996.

75 I devote this column to the Interlog affair, with more space than usual because what happened in Adelaide raises important questions for all organisations employing skilled people and we are not just talking about large enterprises.

Review Exercise B

The writers of all the passages below had the same goal – to attract foreign students to their English language school.
First, give every passage a Global English grade from A-E. (A= Excellent, B=Good, C=OK, D=Poor, E=Very poor)

Secondly, write a few comments about each passage. What aspects of writing style would influence commercial success?

76 We are determined to see this College continue as a school that graduates young men and women who are able to go out to meet a changing and uncertain world with self-confidence based on secure foundations of intellectual ability, a range of useful skills and a set of sound values.

77 Few Colleges offer such a strong curriculum, such wide activities, such outstanding facilities and most importantly such a top-line staff.

78 General Description Of The School

The school consists of some 650 students with approximately 50% male/ 50% female. The junior school (Form 3 and 4) accounts for half the school roll and the fifth form has in recent years been the single largest group of students.

79 Students have regular lessons with an ESOL teacher employed by the school. After the initial orientation unit, the students work on the English language at their particular level e.g. some do Correspondence English, others work towards ESOL Pitman written and oral exams or other relevant courses.

80 Study In Peace

We in New Zealand are friendly and hospitable. We also speak English. Our country is one of the most beautiful in the South Pacific. The landscape is green and fresh, the beaches clean and uncrowded. New Zealand is nuclear-free. We believe there is no nicer or safer place in the world to study.

81 Friendly, Professional Teachers

The friendly teaching staff are all university graduates and ESL qualified. Their wide experience and strong academic backgrounds combine with excellent communication abilities and an understanding of specialty areas such as commerce and business.

82 Enrolment Procedure

1. Contact your agent or the Academy direct for an enrolment form and fees schedule.
2. Send your enrolment form and fees to your agent or to the Academy.
3. When you receive a letter of enrolment and an official receipt, you can apply for a student visa.

83 The International Relations Department welcomes students who wish to major in International Relations but is equally interested in those students who want to take just a few of the available papers, or those who wish to advance two areas of concentration e.g. International Relations and International Business Studies, or International Relations and International Environmental Studies.

84 Learning English has never been easier

Come and study with us in clean fresh surroundings, just 20 minutes from the heart of New Zealand's capital city, Wellington. Full-time and part-time study opportunities are available. Meet new friends among the 1200 other full-time students on campus and enjoy our new student services facilities.

85 What Happens when I Arrive?

You will be assessed with a written test and an interview. Your classes will begin immediately.

What will I be Studying?

All levels include a study of reading, writing, speaking and listening. Pronunciation, grammar, notetaking, conversation skills, comprehension and vocabulary building are examples of some of the topics we cover. We believe listening and speaking are skill areas that need particular emphasis.

86 A New Horizon

The Academy was officially opened in 1988 to provide an educational alternative outside the big cities where students could more easily meet New Zealand people and extend their English through friendships and closer interaction with native English speakers.

The Academy philosophy is based on giving students wide experience of all aspects of spoken English, with extension into practical reading, writing and listening skills that are appropriate to meet the general and academic needs of students.

87 Holiday English

For groups only. These courses generally consist of morning English instruction and afternoon recreational activities such as horse riding and jet boat riding. (Full list of activities on the back of this brochure.) Holiday English courses can be made to suit your group's needs.

88 Entry into any full-time mainstream course by an overseas student is granted providing the student has a TOEFL level of 530 plus or an equivalent English qualification (i.e. IELTS 5-6). Entry can be gained upon completion of an English Language course at Metropolitan Polytechnic on recommendation from the English Language Department.

89 Study English in Auckland, New Zealand's City Of Sails!

Situated between two natural harbours, Auckland is New Zealand's largest city and has many beautiful beaches and parks. The climate is mild and pleasant so you can enjoy an outdoor lifestyle throughout the year.

Review Exercise C

90 *Write a better version of the advertisement below. Follow the principles of Global English. Consider language, structure and layout.*

FINANCE DIRECTOR – CHINA OPERATIONS

Leading Telecommunications Company

Our client, a multinational communications company, with operations around the world, wishes to recruit a Finance Director to head its operations in China.

Based in Hong Kong and reporting to the Chief Financial Officer in the US, core duties will include responsibility for the provision of on-site support to the company's joint ventures and to integrate with the US based reporting group. These activities will include, the development and implementation of accounting systems including internal controls, internal and external reporting, financial planning for Budgets, Forecasts, P & L and new business expansion. Furthermore as a member of the core management team, the Finance Director will be expected to develop a strong, reliable finance team.

Candidates, at least 30 years of age and fluent in Cantonese and English, will be professionally qualified Accountants with approximately 5-10 years proven finance exposure in a subscriber based or telecommunications industry. Important is a combination of public accounting and private industry background, proven man-management skills and an indepth PC knowledge. Ideally, the preferred applicant will be a self starter with the ability to identify and solve problems, exhibit excellent business acumen, strength in integrity, well refined communication and negotiation abilities and a natural capacity to interact effectively at all levels.

Apply to Mr. Tom Jones at the address below, or by fax to 1234-5678.

TS 7890 Alliance Human Resources Consulting Ltd. 8/F, Novam Building, Hong Kong